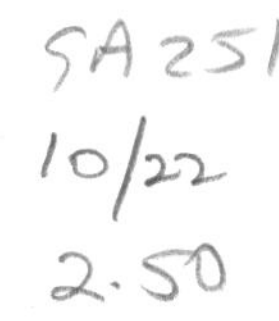

TRAVEL BACK IN THE DAY TO 1972

A Year that Introduced the Memorable Music, Classic Cars and Groovy Fashion Trends We All Know and Love

DAVID & LAUREN BENSON

TRAVEL BACK IN THE DAY TO 1972
A Year that Introduced the Memorable Music, Classic Cars and Groovy Fashion Trends We All Know and Love

DAVID & LAUREN BENSON

Printed in the United States of America
First Printing 2021
First Edition 2021

10 9 8 7 6 5 4 3 2 1

1972

A Special Year For…

Table of Contents

A Special Gift To Our Readers

Included with your purchase of this book is our Travel Back in the Day Trivia. Feel free to download or print these fun-fact questions for you and your friends and test your knowledge of the Year 1972.

Visit the website below and let us know which email address to deliver it to. Enjoy!

backinthedaybooks.com

It's 1972. Whether you were a newborn baby, a newlywed couple, or a graduate from the Class of 1972; this was a special year for you in some significant way.

So let us revisit 1972—a year that kick-started an iconic decade, the era that brought us colorful fashion, unforgettable music, and major global events. The pages to follow are a celebration of all things 1972, you included, and the amazing memories that shaped this year. For you and your own special story this year, let us honor and remember it by taking a nostalgic journey into the year of 1972.

Overview of 1972

1972 Cost of Living

Average Cost of New House	$27,600
Average Cost of New Car	$3,879
Ford Q Code Grand Torino Sport	$4,200
Chevrolet C10 Cheyenne Pickup	$2,680
Gallon of Gasoline	36¢
Postage Stamp	8¢
Movie Ticket	$1.70
Bread	27¢
1lb of Butter	88¢
Gallon of Milk	97¢
A Dozen Eggs	64¢
Bacon	97¢
Men's Print Shirt	$6.99
Women's Jeans	$8.00

1972 Average Income & Salaries

Minimum Wage	$1.60 / Hour
Average Income	$11,116 / Year
Clerical	$6,394 / Year
Manufacturing	$8,045 / Year
State & Local Gov. Employee	$8,900 / Year
Retail Employee	$9,350 / Year
Coal Miner	$9,835 / Year
School Teacher	$10,174 / Year
Construction	$11,501 / Year
Senator	$42,500 / Year
Vice President	$62,500 / Year
President	$200,000 / Year

POPULATION STATISTICS

1972 World Population

Total	3.8 billion

U.S World Population

Total	209.9 million
Male	103.3 million
Female	106.6 million

U.S World Population by Age

Under 1 year	3.3 million
1-4 years	13.8 million
5-14 years	40 million
15-24 years	38.1 million
25-34 years	27.5 million
35-44 years	22.7 million
45-54 years	23.7 million
55-64 years	19.2 million
65-74 years	13 million
75-84 years	7 million
84+ years	1.5 million

UK Population

Total	56.2 million
Male	27.3 million
Female	28.9 million

Canada Population

Total	22.2 million
Male	11.1 million
Female	11.1 million

Australia Population

Total	13.2 million
Male	6.6 million
Female	6.6 million

Chapter 1: Family Life

The wholesome desire and drive for the American dream was now being lived out by the Baby Boomer generation. Newlyweds were congratulated with rice being tossed and shared their first dance to songs like Al Green's "Let's Stay Together" and "Lean on Me" by Bill Withers.

Kathy and Larry's wedding on June 6th, 1972

A total of 1.7 million couples in the US were married this year at the average age of 23 for men and 21 for women. By contrast, 4 out of every 1,000 of these marriages would end in divorce, as no-fault divorce laws were being passed that allowed couples to divorce without legally needing to provide a reason.

Nonetheless, the majority of couples stayed together and started families. 3.3 million babies were born with 1.7 million of them male and 1.6 million female, adding to the 65 million born of Generation X between 1965-1980.

Phyllis and her baby brother in 1972

Top Baby Names in 1972

Male	Female
1. Michael	1. Jennifer
2. Christopher	2. Michelle
3. James	3. Lisa
4. David	4. Kimberly
5. John	5. Amy
6. Robert	6. Angela
7. Jason	7. Melissa
8. Brian	8. Stephanie
9. William	9. Heather
10. Matthew	10. Nicole

HOLIDAYS

John and his Mom putting up the Christmas Tree, December 1971

Fort Sill US Army post in Oklahoma, December 1971

Top Toys of 1972

Cozy winter holidays are always a special time of year for quality time spent with family. Whether you celebrate Christmas, Hanukkah or Kwanzaa, sharing presents with the kiddos and watching their faces light up with glee is simply priceless. Let's check out what toys parents were scrambling to buy and put a price tag on those priceless moments.

Fisher Price Farm Set

Fisher Price by this time had a variety of their "Little People" playsets, but what made this playset so special is that it was the first of their "Play and Carry" sets in which children could easily put away the toy pieces and carry the set by a handle. Originally introduced in 1968 and priced at just under $10 in 1972, a vintage set could sell for as much as $150 today with all parts included.

Toss Across

New life was given to the ol' pen and paper tic-tac-toe game when Toss Across was released in 1969. This version upped the stakes, allowing players to knock off their opponents bean bag, making for a more challenging and competitive game of tic-tac-toe. Originally released by Ideal Toy Company, Toss Across was later acquired by Mattel and is still sold today for just under $20.

Talky Crissy

Talky Crissy was the third of the Crissy doll series, adding to a line of dolls with life-like features such as adjustable hair length, groovy swivel-dance hips and now the ability to talk. Talky Chrissy had many upbeat phrases like "That sounds like fun!", "Let's have a party!" and "I like to dress up!". Originally priced at $13, a mint condition Talky Crissy could sell for as much as $120 today.

Uno

Invented by small-town resident Merle Robins of Reading, Ohio in 1971, Uno quickly became a staple among his friends and family. Merle then invested $8,000 to have 5,000 copies made which sold quickly from his barbershop and other local businesses. In 1972, he sold the rights to Uno to International Games for $50,000 with 10 cents per copy in royalties. Now owned by Mattel, Uno continues to be a friends and family favorite, selling over 151 million copies per year worldwide in 80 countries.

Easy Bake Oven

First released in 1963, the 1972 Easy Bake Oven debuted with a groovy new look and marketing alongside Betty Crocker desserts. Over 500,000 units were sold in their first year and reached 5 million in sales by 1972. A special edition Easy Bake Oven was awarded to the lucky winner of their "5 millionth Easy Bake Oven Sweepstakes". Originally priced at $10.99, the first edition sells the highest today at over $200.

Cooking & Food

Now for a real oven, a gas grill oven at that. This baby baked chocolate cakes, crab legs and steak—talk about an outdoor buffet! Sharing delicious food is one of the best ways to bring family together. From fresh baked pies to carefully crafted cookies, a 70s kitchen always had something good cookin' within those orange colored walls and pea green cabinets.

VACATION

Disney World, having first opened its doors October 1st of 1971, celebrated their first year anniversary in 1972. Over 400,000 new guests were welcomed to enjoy debut exhibits like the Magic Kingdom, Haunted Mansion and Country Bear Jamboree—all still much loved and frequented today. Admission to the park was $3.75 each which included the Disney World Transportation system, Magic Kingdom theme park as well as all their free shows and entertainment. As for the rides, these were a separate cost, but you could purchase an "Eleven Attractions Ticket Book" to ride their top rides for $5.75 each. Overall, a family of 4 could enjoy the day, rides and food included for $10 per person.. compare that to over $100 per person today!

Disney World Magic Kingdom, Orlando, Florida 1977

Fantasyland at Magic Kingdom, Orlando, Florida 1972

By 1972, KOA (Kampgrounds of America) had over 600 campgrounds across the US and Canada. Family and friends around the world enjoyed the great outdoors in their RV's and pop-up campers.

Friends camping in the Rocky Mountains, May of 1972 (photo by Boyd Norton)

1976 Holiday Rambler RV

Notable RV brands of the 70s like Winnebago and Airstream remain popular today for a renovated vintage look. Motels like Holiday Inn and Best Western had revamped their look in the 1970s to accommodate emerging tourist spots for weekend getaways. Many of these tourist spots, such as the San Diego Zoo and Kennedy Space Center, were located near suburbs for families to easily take short trips to.

Family camping at Mt. Madonna, California, 1970

Chapter 2: The Youth of 1972

Education

During this time, there was a growing focus on equality for all. Evidence of this was seen in the changes taking place in the education system. New policies were written to help end segregation and other inequality issues. This led to predominantly white schools seeing greater numbers of minorities in attendance, which then led to greater numbers of minorities receiving higher education later on. Other efforts included bilingual instruction for non-native English speakers, assistance for the disabled, and resources for women to find more employment opportunities in academia.

Elementary School classroom in 1972

High School Graduation Rates

Graduation rates steadily improved throughout the 70s, with about a 75% high school graduation rate overall. In 1972, nearly 3 million high school students graduated, with 1.4 million of them male and 1.5 million female.

High School Prom 1972

Nowadays, the graduation rate is around 86%. Current graduation rates by gender are around 80% for males and 87% for females.

Freshman homeroom at Maryvale High school, 1972

College

In 1972, a landmark education equality bill was passed into law, called Title IX. It made it illegal to discriminate against anyone based on sex in any federally funded educational programs.

The Pell Grant was also created this year. It is the largest grant program offered by the Department of Education to undergraduate students, and is still helping people receive their higher education today.

One of the most notable academic achievements this year was by Willie Hobbs Moore. Moore was the first African-American woman to earn a Ph.D. in Physics in 1972 from the University of Michigan. Her accomplishment inspired many other African-Americans and women alike to strive for a higher education.

In 1972, 1.5 million people enrolled in college with 750,000 male and 709,000 female. Compare that to the total enrollment of college students in 2015 with nearly 19 million enrolled.

Rhodes College in the 1970's (photo by Ed Uthman)

(photo by Ed Uthman)

(photo by Ed Uthman)

PROTESTS

For young adults, especially university students, there was plenty of turbulence for the passionate to get involved in during the 60s and 70s. The major matter of contention was the Vietnam War. Even before the war began in 1954 there were protests, and by 1972 the anti-war movement was well established.

Anti-Vietnam War Protest by students in Paris, 1972

This year saw much controversy, with protests over the Vietnam War occurring at universities around the country and civil rights movements in full swing. Young people were taking to the streets and making their opinions known.

Anti-Vietnam War March in Boston, 1972 (photo by © the Nick DeWolf Foundation)

There was a particularly chaotic protest at the University of Minnesota between May 8th to the 16th, with 3,000 protestors occupying the nearby student neighborhood of Dinkytown. There they faced off with police from seven different counties and 800 National Guardsmen. A make-shift barrier was erected, a car overturned, and building vandalized. 33 people were arrested and 27 people were hospitalized for injuries.

One organization born out of these anti-war sentiments, Greenpeace (renamed from the "Don't Make a Wave Committee" in 1972) saw one of its first acts in 1972 when they sailed to Moruroa (French Polynesia) to disrupt nuclear testing that was being done in the area. The grassroots organization focuses on environmental issues like climate change, protecting biodiversity, and advocating for global disarmament and nonviolence.

Starting out as "an unlikely group of loosely organized protestors", Greenpeace now has offices in over 55 countries around the world.

Korea Peace Corps Volunteers in Suwon, South Korea, 1972

The Hippie Movement's Impact on Society

Although the hippie movement was waning a bit around this time, its influence was still relevant to societal issues like the Vietnam War, because of its emphasis on peace and counterculture. The hippie movement left its mark, and its influences can be seen in music festivals, fashion, and other subculture "peace" movements during 1972. Its presence has had a lasting influence, even in current times. Keep the peace & love, man.

The band "Love Family" performs at a market in Seattle, Washington, 1972

Hippie Commune in 1972 (photo by Ted Pilger)

LSD AND MARIJUANA

According to a Gallup poll, marijuana use was on the rise, with 51 percent of college students saying that they had tried it at least once (1,063 college and university students on 57 campuses were surveyed). Compare that to 1967, when only 5 percent of students said that they had tried it once.

Girls smoking marijuana in Cedar Woods near Leakey, Texas in 1973

Invented in 1938, an estimated 1 to 2 million Americans had taken LSD by 1970. Steve Jobs once said that experimenting with LSD was one of the "two or three most important things" he ever did in his life. Jobs first tried LSD in 1972, during his senior year in high school, and credits his experiences with the psychedelic to seeing the world in new creative perspectives.

The vast majority of people did not use LSD, but that did not mean that it's influence did not make a huge impact, even on mainstream culture. Psychedelic rock was something even the Beatles experimented with, and the strange and mystifying patterns of psychedelic art are well known.

Chapter 3: World Events

World Leaders

- *President Richard Nixon – President of the United States of America*

- *Leonid Brezhnev – General Secretary of the Soviet Union Communist Party*
- *Chairman Mao Zedong – People's Republic of China*

- *Willy Brandt – Chancellor of the Federal Republic of Germany*

• *Indira Gandhi – Prime Minister of India, first and only woman*

• *Kakuei Tanaka – Prime Minister of Japan*

• *President Georges Pompidou – President of France*

• *Pierre Trudeau – Prime Minister of Canada*

• *Edward Heath - Prime Minister of UK*

VIETNAM WAR & PROTESTS

The Vietnam War entered into its 17th year in 1972. December 7th saw the last men to be drafted into service, before drafting officially ended on January 27th, 1973. In Vietnam and at home, sentiments towards the war had soured greatly. Breakdown of order for troops occurred, as many soldiers' outright disobeyed orders or faked reports, losing faith in what was being asked of them. Mass draft evasions were also ongoing throughout the entirety of the war. At home protests continued to rage across the country, as the US slowly reduced its involvement in the war.

THE WATERGATE SCANDAL

5 People were arrested on June 17, 1972 in Washington, D.C for breaking-in to the Democratic National Committee headquarters located in the Watergate Office Building. Investigations uncovered a link between money given to perpetrators and the Nixon re-election campaign committee. Witnesses also testified that Nixon approved plans to cover up his administration's involvement with the break-in. What followed in the next couple of years, has become infamously known as the Watergate Scandal, a multitude of covert and often illegal activities that the Nixon administration was involved in, such as bugging offices of political opponents, investigating activist groups and political figures, and using the FBI, CIA, and IRS as political tools against their opponents. President Nixon eventually resigned in 1974, under growing certainty that his impeachment was inevitable.

Aerial View of the Watergate building in 2008

Moon Landing

Apollo 17 launched on December 7, 1972 and landed on the moon December 11th 2:55 EST. This was the last time any human has been on the moon. The mission was carried out by Commander Eugene Cernan, Lunar Module Pilot Harrison Schmitt, and Command Module Pilot Ronald Evans. It was the longest mission to the moon, taking 12 days from launch to splash down back on earth. It also was the most scientifically intensive, having the first scientist (Harrison Schmitt) on an Apollo mission, carrying out many scientific studies and bringing back more space rock than any other mission. Another record for this mission is having the longest distance traveled using a lunar rover. They traveled a total distance of 20 miles, and got as far as 5 miles away from the mission camp. One of the most famous pictures of the Earth came from this mission. It is known as the Blue Marble, and it is gorgeous.

BLOODY SUNDAY

On Sunday January 30th, 1972 in Derry, Northern Ireland, as many as 15,000 people gathered in the area, protesting the policy of internment, which allowed authorities to imprison suspected IRA (Irish Republican Army) members without trial. The protest march, organized by the Northern Ireland Civil Rights Association, was technically illegal because of a ban on large gatherings, but that would not stop the passionate protestors. Tensions escalated throughout the day, and resulted in British soldiers opening fire on unarmed civilians, 14 people were killed.

Bloody Sunday Memorial March in Derry, Northern Ireland 2007

SHOICHI YOKOI

Japanese holdouts were soldiers of the Japanese imperial army that refused to come home or continued to fight World War II after Japan surrendered in August 1945. Shoichi Yokoi was a Japanese soldier who was found in 1972 in the forests of Guam. He survived on wild nuts, mangos, papaya, shrimp, snails, frogs and rats. He apparently knew since 1952 that the war had ended, but explained, "We Japanese soldiers were told to prefer death to the disgrace of getting captured alive.". After returning to Japan he married (also in 1972!) and even became a popular television personality.

Pierre Hotel Robbery

On January 2nd, one of the largest hotel robberies in history went off without a hitch. Eight disguised men, some professional burglars, others part of the Mafia, managed to rob the Pierre Hotel in New York City and make off with around $3 million dollars (equal to $27 million today) worth of jewelry and cash. However, they didn't really get to enjoy it, as later drama and vengeance saw some of the burglars killed or with a smaller cut of the profit than expected.

Equal Rights Amendment

Women's Strike for Equality demonstration in 1972

In 1972, the Equal Rights Amendment was approved by the Senate, starting the next process of state ratification. The Amendment was first introduced in 1923 and was designed to guarantee equal legal rights for all American citizens regardless of sex. It sought to end the legal distinctions between men and women in terms of divorce, property, employment and any relative matters.

MUNICH OLYMPIC MASSACRE

During the 1972 Summer Olympics, a Palestinian terrorist group calling itself Black September, took nine members of the Israeli Olympic team hostage. A total of 17 people were killed (5 perpetrators and 12 victims).

TECHNOLOGY

Atari releases their arcade version of Pong—the first commercially successful video game. It was a very basic ping-pong style game, in which a ball is bounced back and forth with each player trying to get the other to miss.

Hewlett-Packard introduces the world's first pocket scientific calculator, called the HP-35. A scientific calculator is designed to solve the more complex problems of science, engineering and mathematics, with more features and advanced functions beyond addition, multiplication, subtraction, and division.

Polaroid releases its SX-70 instant film camera, which was an upgrade from previous models. It featured a compact folding design, manual focus, and quicker, less messy developing (within 10 mins).

Andy Warhol taking Polaroid photos with Jack Ford and Bianca Jagger in 1975

Chapter 4: Fashion Trends

What is more iconic and recognizable than the fashion trends of the 1970s? Bright colors, bell-bottom jeans, and eye-catching patterns were fast growing in popularity. It was a much needed overhaul for fashion compared to the more conservative looks of the 50s and 60s.

A Renaissance of sorts it was indeed, and everyone was eager to express themselves creatively through this new variety of clothing. The groovy psychedelic influence of 70s music poured into fashion—making for some pretty off-beat looks, not all of which stood the test of time.

But many of which did and are still seen in the influence of fashion today. High- waisted pants, braless worn tops and oversized glasses remain a fashion staple for women.

GOSPEL MUSIC

As for the men, can't say the bell-bottoms or platform shoes carried over so much, but a classic jacket and low crew-neck top or turtle neck definitely has.

There were a lot more fabrics being produced to choose from that were inexpensive and easy to maintain. Non-iron wool and polyester didn't wrinkle like cotton or linen did, adding to the more casual demeanor of the 70s. Other synthetic fibers like nylon, acrylic and rayon also became more commonly worn. Casual denim jeans challenged the much loved tailored look of dress pants, but corduroy pants were always a nice balance of both looks.

But nothing shined like that super shiny disco clothing, Qiana, a silk-like polyester fabric.

So let's entertain the thought of what walking through the streets in 1972 was like and take a look at what kind of styles everyone was wearing as they passed.

BABY / TODDLER

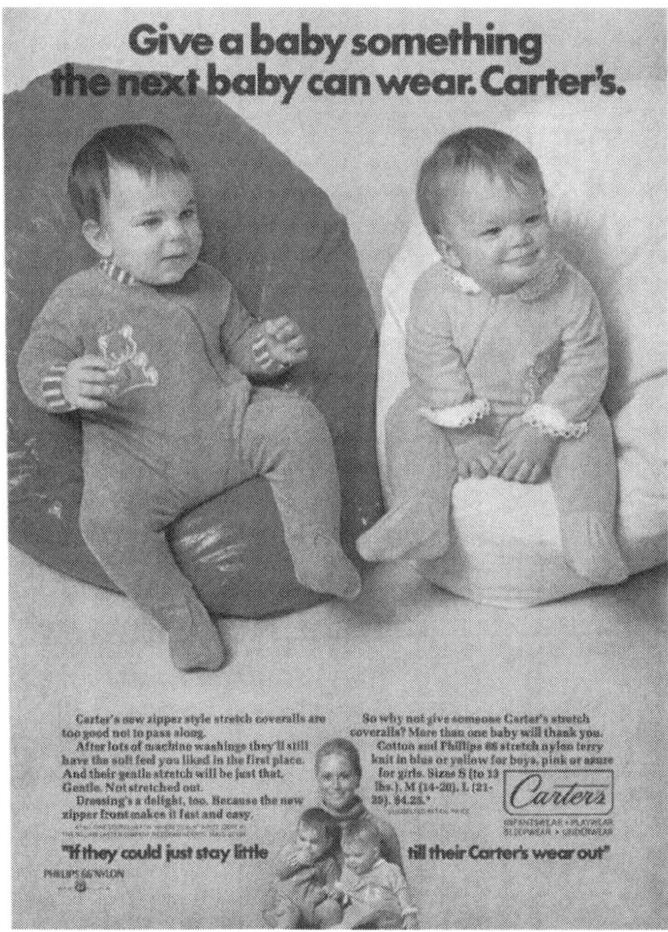

The little ones strutted timeless onesies, well sat in their onesies until they could strut. Favorite cartoon characters on PJ's became more commonly worn, which you bet boosted those TV ratings and toy sales. Parents became more vigilant of what chemicals were in these PJ's and only bought ones with the "flame resistant" label.

GIRLS

Plaid was very popular, especially for young girls who wore plaid everything from the pants, shirts, dresses and skirts. Gingham was also a type of plaid often worn that was a stripe or checkered pattern. Colors were earthy, bold and bright. Jumpers and stockings often made for a dolled up school uniform type look.

Girls on their way home from school in Staten, Island 1973

Boys

Many options for a cool casual look were worn by the boys like a nylon or jean jacket paired with bell-bottoms. Popular cowboy looks were fresh off the farm with boots, hat and all. Vest and bell-bottom sets whether stripped, checkered or plaid were another signature look for the boys.

TEEN GIRLS

Sweet Flares and Body Suits

1 **Button-front Body Suit.** Ribbed knit stretch nylon. Snap crotch. Short sleeves. Machine wash, warm.
Young Teens' sizes 6J, 8J, 10J, 12J, 14J.
V77 N 6397F–Red V77 N 6398F–White
State size. Shipping wt. 4 oz. $8.99

2 **The basic Belt.** Designed especially for jeans, pants. Smooth leather. Gold-color metal buckle. 1¼-in. width.
Sizes S(fits 22–26 in.); M(27–31 in.).
V77N9223F–White V77N9224F–Brown
V77N9225F–Berry (on facing page)
State size S or M. Wt. 6 oz. $2.99

3 **PERMA-PREST® plaid Pants.** Super wide flare legs are about 33 inches around hem of each leg. Teen boy cut . . rides below natural waistline. Zipper fly front. Front pockets. Belt loops. Red, green, blue, white plaid. Fortrel® polyester and cotton woven for a rich wool look, brushed for softness. Machine wash, warm; tumble dry and no ironing ever.
Young Teens' sizes 6J, 8J, 10J, 12J, 14J.
V77 N 6035F—*State size.* Wt. 14 oz. . $9.99

4 **Zip-front Body Suit.** White collar and cuffs. Long sleeves. Ring pull on zipper. Snap crotch. Rib-knit stretch nylon. Machine wash, warm.

Size M	Fits 4 ft. 11½ in. to 5 ft. 1½ in. tall	Fits girls 95 to 100 lbs.
Size L	Fits 5 ft. 2 in. to 5 ft. 4½ in. tall	Fits girls 100 to 115 lbs.

V77 N 6395F–Lime V77 N 6396F–Navy
State size M or L. Wt. 7 oz. $8.99

5 **The fancy Belt.** Schiffli embroidered yellow, lime and white flowers on navy cotton velveteen belt. Vinyl backing. Gold-color metal pull-through buckle. 1¾-inch width.
Sizes S (fits 22–26 in.); M(27–31 in.).
State size S or M.
V77 N 9222F—Shipping wt. 3 oz. . . . $4.99

6 **Velvet Pants.** Very wide flare legs are about 28 inches around hem of each leg. Teen boy cut . . . rides below natural

Bodysuits were often worn with belted bell-bottom pants. This made for a cool yet clean wrinkle-free look. High-waisted shorts and skirts were also a staple look with a variety of stretch polyester tops. Bohemian styles were also very popular with flower power patterns and knitted ponchos.

Teen Boys

Paisley patterned dress shirts paired with a velour or corduroy vest suit were looks you'd probably see worn by Donny Osmond on stage. Polyester leisure suits were a popular go-to for a special occasion while bell-bottom jeans and a well-fitted shirt or bodysuit opted for a more everyday look.

WOMEN

Oriental kimono tops made an appearance with groovy paisley patterns and pleated pants to match. These exotic looks paired surprisingly well with modern slacks and loafers.

There were a variety of bodysuits from button-down, zippered or open-back. Long skirts and wide-legged pants paired with ruffled silk blouses were a relaxed business casual look. Patterned jumpsuits made for a foxy look on a night out while khaki and jean jumpsuits were the perfect cool and casual combo.

Men

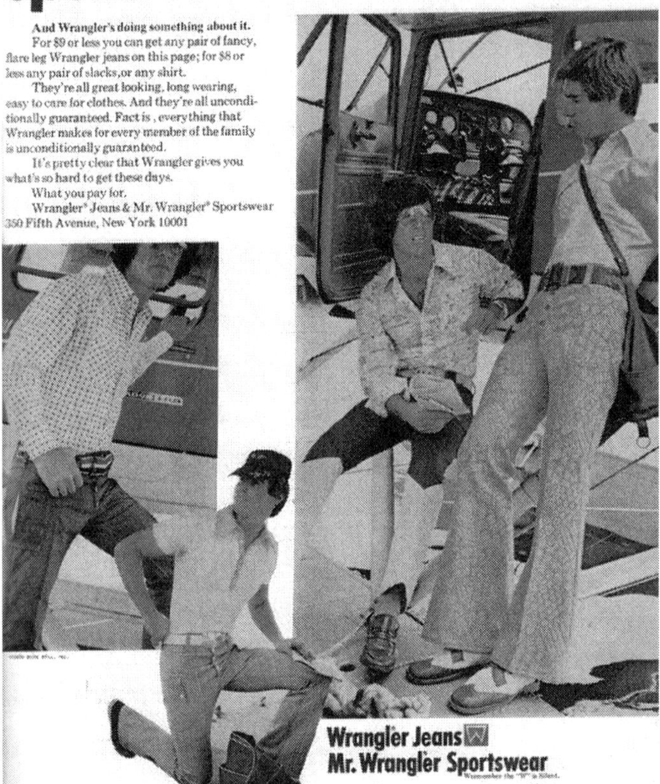

The iconic groovy looks were worn well on men too. Bell bottom pants and funky patterns could be found on the fashionable men of the 70s. A collared dress-shirt unbuttoned with some manly chest hairs showing was a staple look you'd see Sonny Bono singing in with Cher.

Platform shoes were often worn with bell-bottoms that were as high as 4 inches. Other out-there looks uncommonly worn today were belted-sweaters, jumpsuits and bodysuits–those had to have been tight!

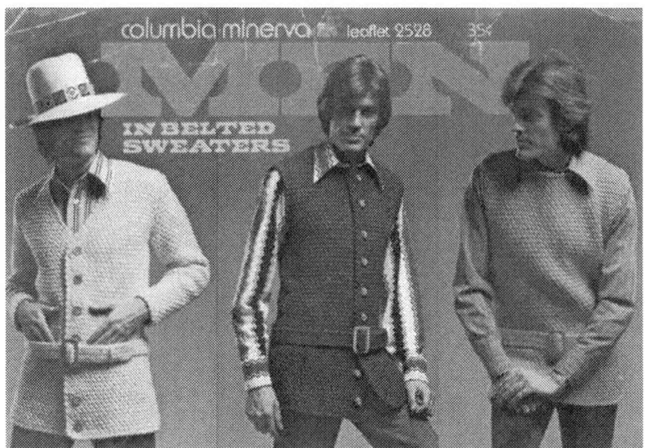

Chapter 5: Music & Entertainment

Student listening to the band "Yes" on campus in 1970

By far one of the best ways to recapture a year in history is by revisiting the music, movies and TV shows that defined the overall cultural vibe of the times. Let's check out what everyone was tuning into on the TV, going to the movies to see and listening to on the radio in their Volkswagen Beetles.

Top 10 TV Shows of 1972

All in the Family held the #1 spot until 1976 since debuting in January of 1971. The show was a favorite among viewers due to its unpolished and relatable depiction of a family and their working-class father, a refreshing shift from shows of the 60s like *Leave it to Beaver* that were much more refined. The show did not shy away from shedding light on life's heaviest challenges, surrounding topics like the Vietnam War, racism and women's liberation while still offering hope, resolution and comedic-relief.

Sanford and Son debuted in 1972 and set the stage for many future African-American sitcoms. The show follows the life of a father and son and their second hand business as they navigate various struggles of their everyday life and relationship, yet find common ground in their shared humorous and upbeat attitudes. Against the odds of being placed in the low view "Friday night death slot", the show still landed #2 highest rated in rank.

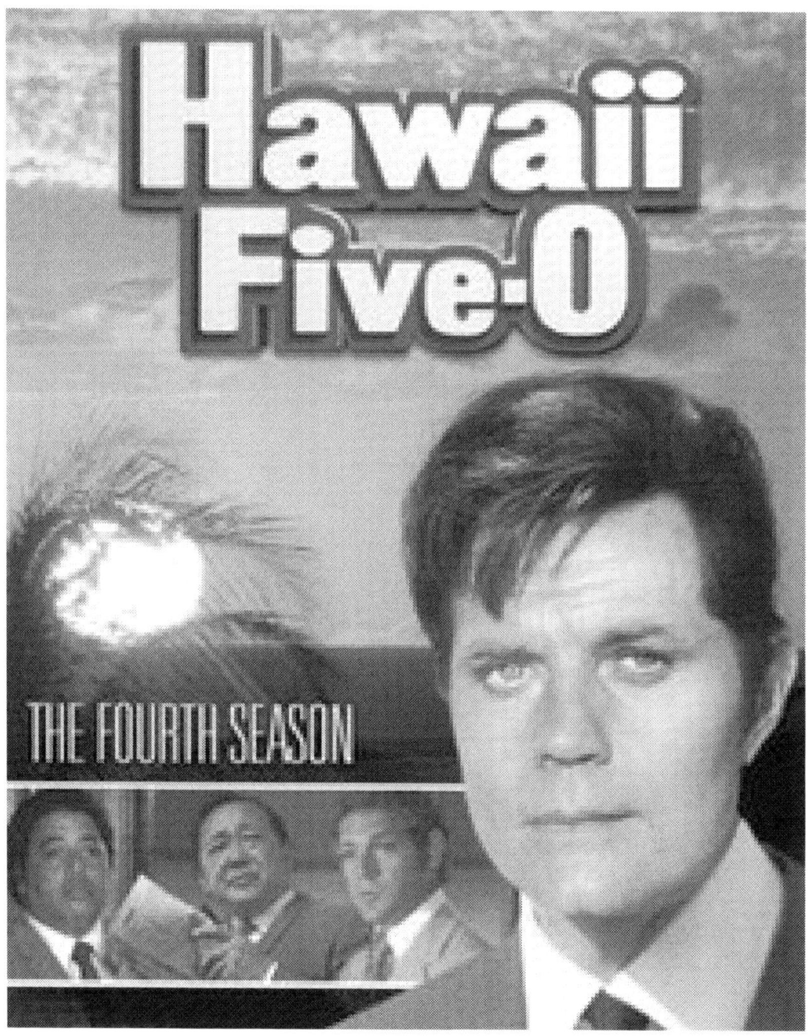

Hawaii Five-0 remains a well-known police crime drama that since airing in 1968 has been widely adapted. The show offered scenic action takes shot in Honolulu, Hawaii filled with suspense and an on-screen team of international secret agents. The original crime series ran from 1968-1980, making it the first of its kind to run for over a decade.

Maude, having had its debut in 1972, was a spin-off of *All in the Family* where this sassy feminist character had made two former guest appearances. Maude gave a platform to women on current world issues like abortion, women's liberation and gender equality with frankness and flair. The show was a controversial comedy that didn't shy away from conflict, much like the main character Maude herself.

Bridget Loves Bernie only ran for a year after its debut in 1972, which was unexpected given its exceptional ratings. The show was about a couple from different religious backgrounds, one of theirs being Jewish and the other Catholic and how they navigated this dynamic. To this day the show remains the highest-rated show to ever have been canceled after only one season.

The NBC Sunday Murder Mystery was a rotating series that aired on Wendesdays and Sundays. Their most popular and well-known series was *Columbo* in which the main character, Lieutenant Columbo, was a homicide detective in Los Angeles known for his quirky demeanor and clever case-closing mind. The show's cliff-hangers and suspenseful storylines kept the show running strong until 1977.

The Mary Tyler Moore Show aired from 1970-1977 and starred actress Mary Tyler Moore who played a driven single woman who worked as a producer of a news program. The show was ground-breaking for it's time as it highlighted a woman who was neither married nor financially dependent on a man— a testament to the Women's Liberation Movement (WLM) during this time. The show received many accolades and is still widely-recognized for its candid comedy and social impact.

Gunsmoke aired in 1955 and remained on air for 20 years until 1975, accumulating a total of 635 episodes. The show was a Western drama that took place in the 1870s and entertained viewers with Wild West gun fast draws, sentimental backstories and a gruff but lovable cast of cowboys and their lady saloon owner friend. The network decided to cancel Gunsmoke unexpectedly so there was unfortunately no season finale episode.

Originally created in 1954 to promote the Disneyland amusement park, **The Wonderful World of Disney** was an evolved version of the show that aired every Sunday until viewership declined in 1975 when 60 minutes premiered on a competing network at the same time. The show featured wholesome family movies like "The Family Band" and "High Flying Spy" which were split into as many as 3 parts shown each weekend.

Ironside was a detective fiction crime drama that aired in 1967 until 1975. The show followed the daily life of a chief detective from San Francisco who was injured on the job, causing him to lose his ability to walk. With resilience, he positioned himself as a special consultant and proved to be an invaluable part of the police department. This lead was played by Raymond Burr, a Canadian-American actor who won six Emmy awards for his role as "Chief Ironside".

24TH EMMY AWARDS

Outstanding Comedy Series: The Carol Bernett Show

Outstanding Drama Series: Elizabeth R Masterpiece Theatre

Outstanding Variety Talk Series: The Dick Cavett Show

TOP 10 MOVIES OF 1972

Based on the best-selling 1969 novel, **The Godfather** remains one of the most recognized movies of its time that received 5 Golden Globe wins in 1973. The storyline of the mob drama is centered around the son of an Italian-American crime boss who joins the mafia and is faced with a harsh reality of violence and sacrifice. The movie had two sequels to follow, one that was released shortly after the first in 1974 and the other later released in 1990.

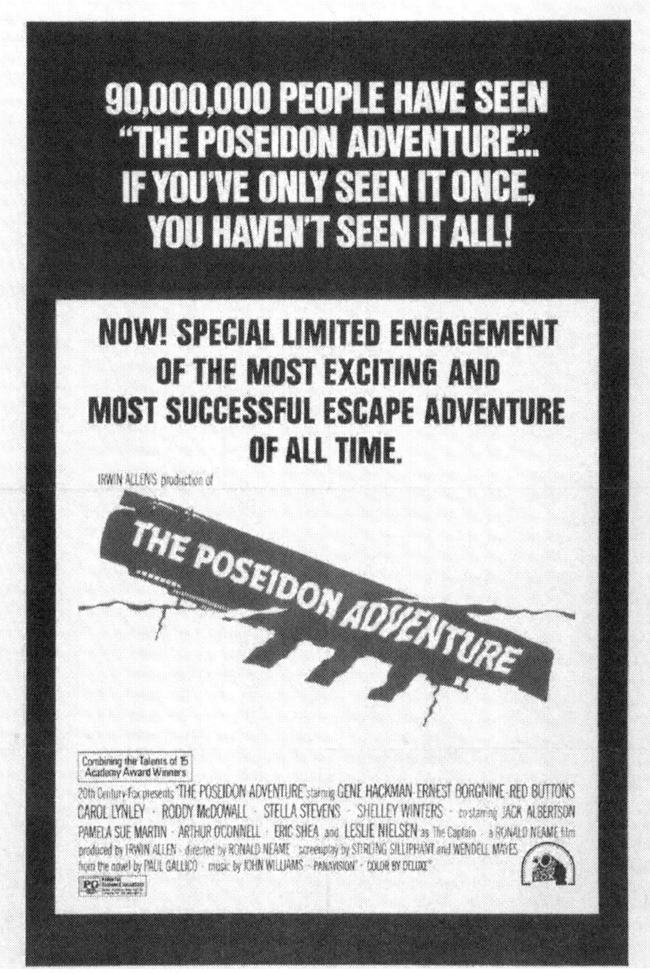

Also based on a novel from 1969, **The Poseidon Adventure** was a disaster film about a luxury ship named the SS Poseidon that is hit by a tsunami, leaving only a group of survivors to find safety. It was the highest grossing film of 1973, having made over $125 million in revenue. The movie was later followed by its sequel *Beyond the Poseidon Adventure* released in 1979.

What's Up Doc was a romantic comedy film starring Barbara Streisand who plays a charming trouble-maker that romances a musicologist in San Francisco and stirs up a whole basket case of adventures. The film was awarded "Best Comedy written Directly for the Screen" by the Writers Guild of America in 1973 and remains a critically acclaimed comedy today by the American Film Institute.

Deliverance was a survival film about four close friends and family men who in an attempt to have a fun trip away from home in rural Georgia, find themselves being attacked by the territorial savages that live in the woods. The film was criticized for its overly graphic scenes but still praised for its memorable music scene moment where one of the men plays the famous bluegrass song "Dueling Banjos" with a local country boy.

Based on a true story about John "Liver-Eating" Johnson, **Jeremiah Johnson** starred Robert Redford as a mountain man and former Mexican-American war veteran. The film inspired movie goers with a riveting story of resilience and survival in the face of many challenges and death-defying experiences. It was featured in the 1972 Cannes Film Festival.

The iconic **Cabaret**, was directed by widely-recognized choreographer and filmmaker Bob Fosse. The movie stars the daughter of Judy Garland, Liza Minnelli and features an eerie look into a racy, wild cabaret that is the source of respite and entertainment as the Nazi regime dawns. The movie takes place in Berlin in 1931 during the Weimar Republic, the former German state and is based on the true story of Sally Bowels, an aspiring cabaret singer of the times.

Deep Throat was a notable film of "porno chic" culture that ran from 1969-1984. While attempting to frame the movie as part of the feminist movement during the 1970s and encourage sexual liberation, it was unfortunately far from it as the lead actress, Linda Lovelace, was sexually assaulted for many of the scenes within the movie. It was shot in less than a week in North Miami and was an hour long movie.

The Getaway was an action thriller based on the 1958 novel about criminals who after a bank heist flee to Mexico and attempt to outrun other cops and competing criminals who are after them in hot pursuit. Farrah Faucet was considered to play the lead female role that Ali MacGraw was ultimately chosen to play by her husband who was an executive at the studio production.

Lady Sings the Blues was a biography about Billie Holiday who was played by singer Diana Ross, who in 1973 won a Golden Globe for "New Star of the Year". The movie was the first African-American biography to be nominated for the Academy Awards and its soundtrack album was number one for two weeks in April of 1973.

Everything You Always Wanted to Know About Sex was a sex comedy directed by Woody Allen adapted from the novel written in 1969. The film was organized into seven sections of peculiar questions and starred Woody Allen himself as well as actor Gene Wilder. The film was rather strange and taboo, having even been banned in Ireland in 1973.

29TH GOLDEN GLOBES

Best Drama Motion Picture: The French Connection

Best Comedy / Musical Motion Picture: Fiddler on the Roof

Best Foreign Film: Sunday Bloody Sunday (United Kingdom)

Best Performance in a Motion Picture Drama:

Actor: Gene Hackman - in The French Connection as Det. Jimmy "Popeye" Doyle

Actress: Jane Fonda- in Klute as Bree Daniels

Best Performance in a Motion Picture Comedy / Musical:

Actor: Chaim Topol in Fiddler on the Roof as Tevye

Actress: Dame Leslie Lawson (Twiggy) in The Boy Friend as Polly Browne

Top 30 Singles of the Year 1972

No.	Title	Artist
1	"The First I Ever Saw Your Face"	Roberta Flack
2	"Alone Again (Naturally)"	Gilbert O'Sullivan
3	"American Pie"	Don McLean
4	"Without You"	Harry Nilsson
5	"The Candy Man"	Sammy Davis Jr.
6	"I Gotcha"	Joe Tex
7	"Lean On Me"	Bill Withers
8	"Baby, Don't Get Hooked On Me"	Mac Davis
9	"Brand New Key"	Melanie
10	"Daddy Don't You Walk So Fast"	Wayne Newton
11	"Let's Stay Together"	Al Green
12	"Brandy (You're a Fine Girl)"	Looking Glass
13	"Oh Girl"	The Chi-Lites
14	"Nice to Be with You"	Gallery
15	"My Ding-a-Ling"	Chuck Berry

16	"(If Loving You is Wrong) I Don't Want to Be Right"	Luther Ingram
17	"Heart of Gold"	Neil Young
18	"Betcha by Golly, Wow"	The Stylistics
19	"I'll Take You There"	The Staple Singers
20	"Ben"	Michael Jackson
21	"The Lion Sleeps Tonight"	Robert John
22	"Outa-Space"	Billy Preston
23	"Slippin' into Darkness"	War
24	"Long Cool Woman in a Black Dress"	The Hollies
25	"How Do You Do"	Mouth & MacNeal
26	"Song Sung Blue"	Neil Diamond
27	"A Horse with No Name"	America
28	"Popcorn"	Hot Butter
29	"Everybody Plays the Fool"	The Main Ingredient
30	"Precious and Few"	Climax

Roberta Flack's "The First I Ever Saw Your Face" placed #1 on the Billboard charts for 6 weeks straight. The song was featured in Clint Eastwood's 1972 movie, *Play Misty for Me* which introduced many to the singer.

Neil Young wrote "Heart of Gold" on his acoustic *Harvest* album after a back injury that made it difficult for him to play on the electric guitar. The song was recorded in February of 1972 in Nashville, Tennessee.

Michael Jackson's "Ben" was based on the 1972 thriller movie *Ben* about a boy who befriends a rat. The heartfelt song was promoted separate from the movie and unbeknownst to many listeners was about a rat.

Al Green's popular wedding song "Let's Stay Together" was featured in several different movies, but perhaps the most notable was its placement in the 1994 film, *Pulp Fiction*. The song placed at #60 of *Rolling Stone's* "Top 500 Songs of All Time".

"I'll Take You There" by The Staple Singers was inspired by Martin Luther King Jr.'s speech to which lead singer Mavis Staples stated; "If he can preach this, we can sing it.". The song spent 15 weeks on the *Billboard* Top 100 in 1972.

America's "A Horse with No Name" was a song lead singer Dewey Burnnell wrote about the desert scenery surrounding the Air Force Base his father was stationed at in Santa Barbara, California. The song was mistaken by many as a Neil Young song when released.

Swedish group ABBA was formed in 1972. The band name was formed by the initials of members Agnetha Fältskog, Björn Ulvaeus, Benny Andersson and Anni-Frid Lyngstad. Their first single, "People Need Love", was recorded this year and its success led them to performing their hit single, "Waterloo", in the 1974 Eurovision Competition and taking home 1st place to Sweden.

David Bowie's *Ziggy Stardust Tour* ran for 191 shows with music off of 3 of his best selling albums. Accompanied by his backup group, "Spiders from Mars", the tour spanned across the UK, US and Japan and received rave reviews for Bowie's wild androgynous costumes and zany story-telling choreography.

Pink Floyd's *Dark Side of the Moon* tour ran for 132 shows from January of 1972 to June of 1973 across the UK, US and Japan. The album was not released until March of 1973, so many concert goers were able to experience this album for the first time live. The album remains the 6th best-selling album of all time, having sold over 45 million copies worldwide.

Ike & Tina Turner were a husband and wife duo who had become a mainstream success in the early 70s. One of their notable R&B hits was a cover of Creedence Clearwater Revival's "Proud Mary" off their 1970 album "Workin' Together". The song earned them a Grammy for "Best R&B Vocal Performance by a Group" in 1972.

15TH ANNUAL GRAMMYS

Record of the Year: "The First Time I Saw Your Face" Roberta Flack

Album of the Year: The Concert for Bangladesh feat. George Harrison, Ravi Shankar, Bob Dylan, Leon Russell, Ringo Starr, Billy Preston, Eric Clapton, and Klaus Voormann

Best New Artist of the Year: America

FAMOUS PEOPLE BORN IN 1972

Actress Jennifer Garner, April 17th

Singer/Songwriter Billie Joe Armstrong, February 17th

Actress Cameron Diaz, August 30th

Rapper Eminem, October 17th

Actress Gwyneth Paltrow, September 27th

Actor Jude Law, December 29th

Actress Leslie Mann, March 26th

Actor Ben Affleck, August 15th

Burlesque Performer Dita Von Teese, September 28th

Singer/Songwriter Rob Thomas, February 14th

Actress Sofia Vergara, July 10th

Basketball Player Shaquille O'Neal, March 6th

Actress Claire Forlani, December 17th

Rapper Notorious B.I.G, May 21st

Actress & Model Jenny McCarthy, November 1st

Actor Dwayne Johnson, May 2nd

Singer & Actress Gerri Halliwell, August 6th

Singer/Songwriter Brad Paisley, October 28th

Actress & Model Carmen Electra, April 20th

Singer/Songwriter Liam Gallagher, September 21st

Actress Amanda Peet, January 11th

Soccer Player Zinedine Zidane, June 23th

Actress Maya Rodolf, June 27th

Producer & Rapper Timbaland, March 10th

CHAPTER 6: SPORTS

WINTER OLYMPICS

This marked the first time the Winter Olympic Games took place outside Europe or North America. It was officially known as the XI Olympic Winter Games, and was held from February 3rd to February 13th, 1972, in Sapporo, Japan. Japan took gold, silver and bronze for ski jumping in a podium sweep. This was also the first time Japan won a gold medal in the Winter Olympics, achieved by Yukio Kasaya.

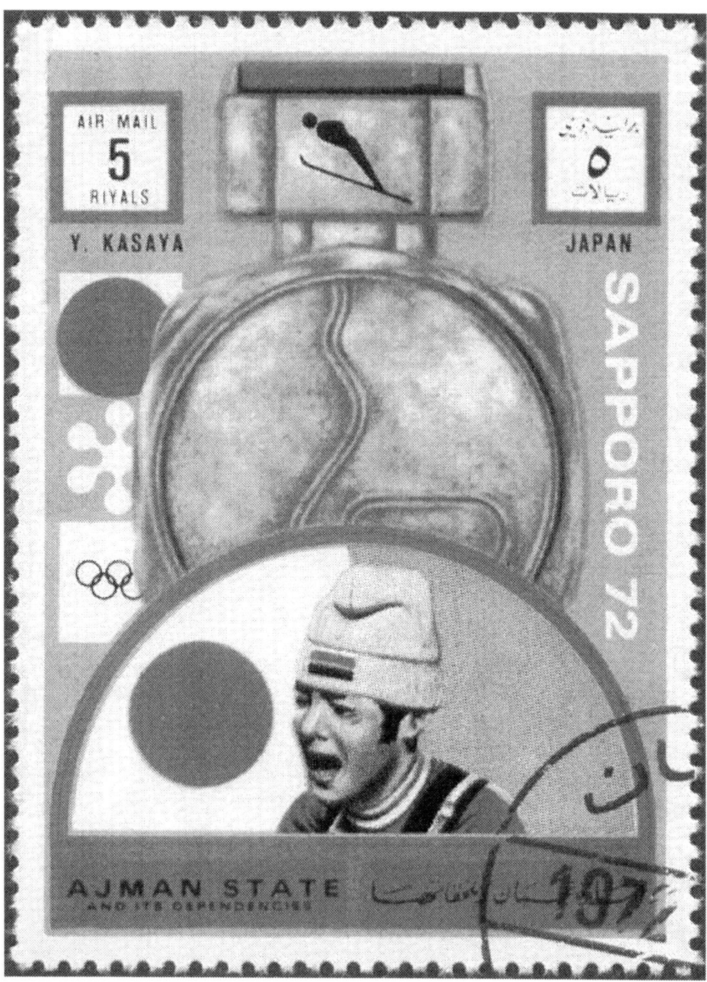

The very last time a skier won a gold medal on all-wooden skis was during these games, ever since then all pro skiers started to move to skis of more modern materials such as fiberglass.

The US Women's Ski Team took home a gold medal when Barbara Cochran won the top spot in Alpine skiing—making her the first US woman to win gold in skiing since 1952. She was one of four siblings on the US skiing team, alongside two of her sisters and one brother. She came from a family of top skiers, her parents, as well as the generation after her own, all being top competitors in major events.

1972 Winter Olympic Medals Won

Rank	Nation	Gold	Silver	Bronze	Total
1	Soviet Union	8	5	3	16
2	East Germany	4	3	7	14
3	Switzerland	4	3	3	10
4	Netherlands	4	3	2	9
5	United States	3	2	3	8
6	West Germany	3	1	1	5
7	Norway	2	5	5	12
8	Italy	2	2	1	5
9	Austria	1	2	2	5
10	Sweden	1	1	2	4
11	Japan	1	1	1	3

SUMMER OLYMPICS

The 1972 Summer Olympics were held in Munich, Bavaria, West Germany, from August 26th to September 11th, 1972. Officially known as the **Games of the XX Olympiad**, they were the 20th games held since the introduction of the modern Olympic games in 1896. The Soviet Union took home the most gold medals, winning 50. The US came in second with 33, East Germany with 20, and West Germany taking home 13.

1972 Summer Olympic Medals Won

Rank	Nation	Gold	Silver	Bronze	Total
1	Soviet Union	50	27	22	99
2	United States	33	31	30	94
3	East Germany	20	23	23	66
4	West Germany	13	11	16	40
5	Japan	13	8	8	29
6	Australia	8	7	2	17
7	Poland	7	5	9	21
8	Hungary	6	13	16	35
9	Bulgaria	6	10	5	21
10	Italy	5	3	10	18

MARK SPITZ

Major Olympic history was made this year. Mark Spitz won 7 gold medals, a feat that would not be topped until 2008 by Michael Phelps. However, Spitz set a new world record in every event he won, and that is something that still has yet to be matched. Spitz was a phenomenal athlete, before the 1972 Olympic games even started, he had already won 2 gold medals (1968 Olympics) and 5 gold medals from the 1967 Pan American Games, as well as already holding 10 world records. He was truly a top athlete that continued to excel.

Olga Korbut

Another standout athlete at the Summer Olympics was the Soviet gymnast Olga Korbut. Her dramatic and daring performances are credited with taking gymnastics from a niche sport to one of the most popular Olympic events. Her likeable charm and acrobatic skill captivated many. One of her performances was so well-received that when she was given a score of 9.8, the crowd began booing, arguing for a perfect score. Being as skilled as she was, she introduced new moves to gymnastics such as her namesakes, the Korbut flip and dismount on the bars, as well as the back flip on beams.

SUMMIT SERIES

The Summit Series, also known as the Canada-USSR Series, was a series of 8 games played between two of the best competing hockey teams from Canada and the Soviet Union. The Cold War was still dragging on and this was an opportunity to have some competitive feelings of nationalism on ice, away from the chaotic political stage. In the beginning the Soviet Union was winning but Canada made a comeback when Paul Henderson scored the winning goal in the last 34 seconds of the 8th game.

FOOTBALL

DALLAS COWBOYS MAKE A COMEBACK

The Dallas Cowboys had a spectacular Super Bowl VI win against the Miami Dolphins at Tulane Stadium in New Orleans on January 16th, 1972 to decide the 1971 season. At the big game, the Cowboys defeated the Dolphins (24-3), and for the next 47 years they would remain the only team to prevent the opposing team from scoring a touchdown during a Super Bowl. They also set some other Super Bowl records, including most rushing yards (252) and most first downs (23).

Miami Dolphins Go Completely Undefeated

During the 1972 season, Miami came back fiercely from this Super Bowl defeat, remaining undefeated for the entire season, this included having won the Super Bowl VII against the Washington Redskins (14-7). To this date, they are the only team to have a perfect undefeated season.

Baseball Strike

1972 saw the first games cancelled due to player strikes over pension and salary arbitration. It went on from April 1st to the 13th. This resulted in the first week and half of the season being erased, and the League decided not to have any make-up games. This caused some uneven scoring in the standings and affected which team made the playoffs.

Carl Yastrzemski (Yaz) plays for the Boston Red Sox in the 1970's (photo by Steven Carter.)

HANK AARON

Here is a legendary Baseball name, Hank "Hammer" Aaron has left an incredible mark on the sport. He hit 24 or more home runs every year from 1955 through 1973, broke Babe Ruth's home run record with 755 in his career, and is among one of two players to hit 30 or more home runs during 15 different seasons each.

The World Series Champions of 1972 were the Oakland Athletics, defeating the Cincinnati Reds (4-3). It was the first time the Athletics were at the World Series championship since 1930.

Championships Overview

Super Bowl VI Champions – Dallas Cowboys defeat Miami Dolphins

NBA Champions – Los Angeles Lakers defeat New York Knicks

Stanley Cup – Boston Bruins win 4 games to 2 over the New York Rangers

U.S. Open Tennis Champions – Ilie Nastase / Billie Jean King

Open Golf Champion – Jack Nicklaus

Wimbledon Tennis Champions – Stan Smith / Billie Jean King

NCAA Football Champions – USC

NCAA Basketball Champions – UCLA

Kentucky Derby – Riva Ridge

Chapter 7: Automobiles

"They don't make 'em like they used to…" is a phrase you could really apply to the cars of the 70s. The cars back then had classy looks, mean muscle, and solid builds. They were often built with more space for large families, and with large motors to move such large, often boat-like sized vehicles.

This all began to shift though after 1972 when in 1973 the US chose to supply Israli troops during the Yom Kippur War. In response, members of OPEC (Organization of the Petroleum Exporting Countries) placed an oil embargo on the US and gas prices rose. More compact, economically friendly cars were built to combat this problem that luckily cleared up by early 1974. Large bumpers were also a buzzkill to the car industry in 1973, and had to be large enough to withstand an impact at 5 mph. This became a bulky challenge for car design makers that they now had to work around.

So 1972 was somewhat of a "calm before the storm" before 1973's automobile industry changes and regulations. Let's take a look at some of these bumperless cars and early models of popular compact cars.

Perhaps an exception to the large cars of the 70s was the VW Beetle. In 1972, this tiny bug became the world's best-selling car. The 15,007,034th Beetle was produced on February 17th, breaking the previous record held by the Ford Model T. It cost $2,000 and according to one ad it could briefly float, although attempting to find out if that was true was probably best avoided. But what it is best known for, is its iconic look. Careful seeing one on the road, they are also known as "punch bugs". No punch backs!

You can't talk about iconic cars and the 70s without mentioning the VW Bus. Highly sought after to this day, this little bus has a lot of charm. 1972 was actually the year VW made some changes to the design. It lost its distinctive split front windshield, became a little bit larger and heavier, and updated the rear axle.

Here's another car that with just a glance you can see how the 70s were a very different era. If a station wagon and a pickup truck had a baby, you would get the Ford Ranchero, a two-door "utility coupe" station wagon with a cargo bed. 1972 saw a design change for the Ranchero, becoming a bit larger and updating the front grille.

A work horse or wild horse? The Ford Bronco got its name from the Spanish term used to describe a cowboy's hard-to-tame horse. It was the first vehicle to be coined as a "Sports-Utility Vehicle" (SUV), making for a useful combination of a pick-up truck and off-roading chick magnet. Sales for 1972 were over 21 thousand units but 1974 was its best-selling year of the 70s, having sold over 26 thousand units.

Ford's marketing hit home with blue collar and homegrown folk, so it made sense to have more than one car named after a horse. The Ford Mustang introduced a new class of cars called "pony cars", which is an affordable sporty coupe or convertible with a long hood and short neck. Other notable pony cars and competitors for the Ford Mustang are the Chevy Camaro and Dodge Challenger.

With the Ford Bronco doing as well as it was, Chevy wanted a piece of the money pie and came out with the Chevy Blazer to stir up some competition. The Chevy Blazer came with an automatic transmission, where the Ford Bronco didn't have this option until its 1973 model. This was the last Chevy Blazer of its first generation model that ran from 1969-1972.

THE BIG CAR
INSIDE OUR
LITTLE CAR.

Into each Vega a little Impala goes.
Power ventilation system.
Front disc brakes.
Side-guard door beams.
Two steel roofs instead of just one.
And, strange as it may seem, Vega's room-per-passenger compares pretty well with Impala's.
But Vega is no big car.
It's made for four people.
And although Vega's low center of gravity and wide stance make it feel bigger than a Vega, it's all done on a modest eight-foot wheelbase. (Two feet less than Impala's.)
Although our overhead-cam aluminum block engine is bigger than most little car engines, it's still awfully stingy with a gallon of gas.
And although Vega, with full foam seats and Full Coil suspension, is surprisingly comfortable to ride in from city to city, it's also a nifty car to zip around in from store to store.
Vega is a little car.
The little car that does everything well.

VEGA
CHEVROLET

CAR CRAFT □ JUNE 1972 67

After winning 1971's *Motor Trend* Car of the Year, the Chevy Vega was selling well after a great first impression. Unfortunately, this was short-lived and by May of 1972, 6 out of 7 Chevy Vega's produced were recalled with all sorts of problems. The name "Vega" was inspired by the name of the brightest star of the Lyra constellation, but it seems this Vega's starlight ended up burning out.

In an effort to be environmentally friendly, this version of the Chrysler Newport Royal had an electric ignition. A higher beltline was also added which made for a more tank-like appearance. The "royal" name didn't quite stick and it was dropped in 1973.

RIDE ON CLOUD 9
WITH MOTOROLA
WRAP-AROUND SOUND
in a 4-channel, 8-track tape player
4 amplifiers and 4 Deluxe 5¼" Golden Voice Speakers matched to circuitry wrap the sound around you. Motorola's TM920S makes turning on a car tape player a whole new happening.
Tool Steel Lock That Defies Hacksaws. Optional.
SIDE TRACK—its face lights up so you can load it in the dark.
It loads from the side instead of the front —designed with safety in mind. Two-channel, 8-track. Model TM717S
GIVES YOU THE WORKS
FM Stereo Radio, 2-channel 8-track tape player, all wrapped up in one attractive package. Model TF800S
TURNS YOUR AM CAR RADIO INTO AM-FM.
Model FM70M adds the pleasure of FM to your 12 volt, negative ground AM car radio.
MOTOROLA®
SOMETHING ELSE in sound on wheels

This was the first Pontiac Grand Am of five generations produced until 2005. All of the 1972-1975 Grand Ams were produced in Pontiac, Michigan. The 1972 version was made to resemble a European luxury/sport sedan while also being good on gas. This confused buyers and it didn't sell as well as they were hoping.

Named after "skylark" birds, this Buick Skylark was a second generation model of a series that ran from 1968-1972. This now included the 350 inch V8 engine in a two-door hardtop coupe or four-door sedan. Their limited production model, the Buick Skylark 350 Sun Coup came complete with a sliding vinyl sunroof.

Just like the Pontiac Grand Am, the Oldsmobile Cutlass S was also made to resemble a European luxury/sport sedan. This 1972 model came complete with a new checkered-square grill and tail lights that were more narrow and triangular. The name "Cutlass" was inspired by the type of sword used by pirates.

Priced slightly above the Volkswagen Beetle at $2,100, the Toyota Celica ST positioned itself to be "more car" than the Beetle for around the same price. It also set out to compete with the Ford Mustang, pricing the Celica at about $500 cheaper. The name "Celica" was inspired by the Latin word "coelica" which means "celestial".

The well-known Toyota Corolla began production in 1966 and is still being produced today, making it the 13th longest-running car models of all time. The name "Corolla" was inspired by the Latin word for "small crown". By 1974 it was "crowned" a small car crown as the best-selling car worldwide.

The less you spend on a car, the more you can spend on other things.

This car gets up to 40 miles to the gallon.

Up to 75 miles an hour.

Overhead cam engine, rack and pinion steering, 4-speed synchromesh transmission, power-assisted front disc brakes, front bucket seats, radial tires, tachometer, racing mirror. All standard equipment.

Oh, it doesn't have automatic transmission, air conditioning, and a 400-horsepower engine.

But which would you rather have? Automatic transmission, air conditioning, and a 400-horsepower engine?

Or Michelle and Tammy and Alison?

The Honda Coupe. $1735.*

It makes a lot of sense.

Due to the 1973 oil crisis, it was important to consumers to be driving something good on gas. The Honda Coupe was made for just that at 40 miles per gallon but didn't offer much of anything else. An automatic transmission and AC were not part of the deal but, being priced below the $2,000 mark, it was an attractive option.

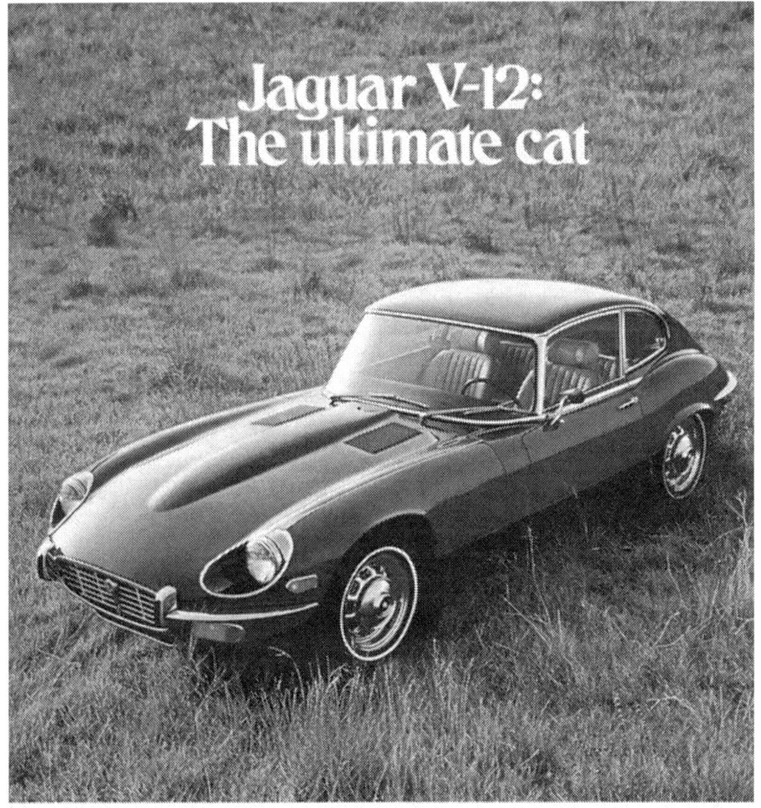

With a top speed of 135 mph, the Jaguar V12 out-sold other competing high-performance cars for its reasonable price point at $7,599, compared to about $12,000 for competing models like the BMW. This iconic car is still much-loved today, having made an appearance in the movie *Austin Powers* and TV show *Mad Men.*

The BMW 3.0 CSL was a bit faster than the Jag with a top speed of 139 mph. This car was not sold in the US but is an honorable mention due to the unique fact it was special-built to be eligible for the European Touring Car Championship. Nicknamed the "batmobile", it impressed many with its bold design and high-speed.

MEMORIES

Here are a few fond memories from our friends and readers,

DAVE COOK

"I saw Pink Floyd in concert in January 1972 at City Hall Newcastle Upon Tyne. Floyd were my absolute favourite band then and I always hoped I'd get to see them play one day. I remember vividly how excited I was on the bus with a couple of mates on the way to Newcastle with our cherished Floyd tickets in our pockets. The atmosphere in the hall was electric, many people were looking at the stage and marveling at the array of gear and lighting the band were using. I'd seen quite a few bands in City Hall, but none of them had the amount of gear Floyd had. They had the giant circular film screen which became a regular feature of their show. It was also in quadraphonic sound, the giant speaker stacks in each corner of the hall, again a first for us. The atmosphere was electric when they came on stage, the sound of massively loud heartbeats coming from the speakers situated behind us. That was the first time everyone in the audience heard those heart beats which would, the following year, open the album Dark Side of the Moon which sold zillions worldwide. The concert was amazing, I was only sixteen, Floyd were my idols back then, I'm still a dedicated fan of their music. They played the epic Echoes as an encore from the Meddle album which came out the previous year. When we all heard Dark side when it was released the following year in 1973, we were staggered at how polished and amazing it sounded with all the sound effects and spoken voices added to the incredible album Dark side of the Moon had evolved into. I still cite that concert as one of the best I've ever seen."

DAVID SWANGER

"Fall of 1972, I was a freshman at Auburn University. First week of class, I bought season football tickets (in the student section for home games). I was about to walk away with my tickets when I realized I could buy a ticket to the Alabama game in Birmingham. I bought the ticket. Late in the fall, I attended the game and Alabama led Auburn 16–3 in the 4th quarter. Auburn returned two blocked Alabama punts for touchdowns and won 17–16. That is a fond memory for me."

DOLORES TRACY

"When I went to the neighborhood park to play and found a stray dog who kept following me home, and became my first dog. Great guard dog. He was a benji dog."

JUDITH JONES

"Hiphugger bellbottoms button front and wedge shoes. And a flat stomach!"

ANN GOODIN

"We adopted our daughter when she was ten days old. I love her to bits and she has been a wonderful daughter."

Do you have a memory you'd like to share?

Or perhaps something new you learned about the year you were born that you found interesting.

We would love to hear and enjoy any feedback or suggestions

you may have.

Your contribution and input in the form of a Review/Star Rating means so much to the future development of books like these for our readers in the years to come.

We hope you enjoyed this nostalgic journey through 1972 and wish you, your friends and family many more special memories to be made together.

Image Attributions

Overview:

Stamp 1972. Source: https://commons.wikimedia.org/wiki/File:Stamp_Collecting_8c_1972_issue_U.S._stamp.jpg. No copyright mark (Public Domain (PD)) image.

Gas Station 1972. Source: https://commons.wikimedia.org/wiki/File:Boron_Gasoline_Station_1972.jpg. No copyright mark (PD image).

Movie Theatre 1972. Source:

https://commons.wikimedia.org/wiki/File:Seattle,_looking_north_on_First_from_Union,_1972.jpg. No copyright mark (PD image).

Family Life:

Marriage photo. Source: https://www.flickr.com/photos/larrywkoester/45199859885/in/photostream/ by Larry Koester. Attribution 4.0 International. (CC by 4.0).

Siblings. Source: https://www.flickr.com/photos/pgautier/157451517 by Phyllis Buchanan. Attribution 4.0 International. (CC by 4.0).

Xmas funny tree. Source: https://www.flickr.com/photos/sillysocks/7708378250/ by Barbara Ann Spengler. Attribution 4.0 International. (CC by 4.0).

Xmas tree. Source: https://www.flickr.com/photos/sillysocks/7708444174/ by Barbara Ann Spengler. Attribution 4.0 International. (CC by 4.0).

Xmas helicopter. Source: https://www.flickr.com/photos/sillysocks/7708364638/ by Barbara Ann Spengler. Attribution 4.0 International. (CC by 4.0).

Fisher Price Farm. Source:

https://www.etsy.com/listing/1005015958/1970s-fisher-price-family-play-farm-915?gpla=1&gao=1&&utm_source=google&utm_medium=cpc&utm_campaign=shopping_us_a-toys_and_games-toys-other&utm_custom1=_k_Cj0KCQjwg7KJBhDyARIsAHrAXaERvTUMlhwN1LB6cWbx6Mh7lwtBeOiuC3ZJ-6CzCvr3smpvHevxPhIaAuO-

EALw_wcB_k_&utm_content=go_1844702853_71423545842_346398441550_pla-314535280500_c__1005015958_469737675&utm_custom2=1844702853&gclid=Cj0KCQjwg7KJBhDyARIsAHrAXaERvTUMlhwN1LB6cWbx6Mh7lwtBeOiuC3ZJ-6CzCvr3smpvHevxPhlaAuO-EALw_wcB. Pre 1978, (PD* image)

Beauty toy doll. Source:

https://www.retrowaste.com/wp-content/gallery/1970s-toys-ads/?C=S;O=A. Pre 1978, (PD* image)

Toss Across. Source:

https://twitter.com/RetroNewsNow/status/944243655338053632/photo/1. Pre 1978, (PD* image)

Easy Bake Oven. Source:

https://www.etsy.com/listing/850692679/1972-kenner-easy-bake-oven-with-original. Pre 1978, (PD* image).

Crissy Talky Doll. Source:

https://www.pinterest.com/pin/567172146791912091/. Pre 1978, (PD* image).

Uno. Source:

https://www.pinterest.com/pin/376543218849018934/. Pre 1978, (PD* image).

Broilmaster. Source: https://www.flickr.com/photos/91591049@N00/31287969310

By SensaAlan. Attribution 4.0 International. (CC by 4.0).

Disney 1972. Source:

https://commons.wikimedia.org/wiki/File:Disneyworld,_Orlando,_FL,_summer_1972_11.jpg. No copyright mark (PD image).

Disney 1972. Source:

https://commons.wikimedia.org/wiki/File:Disneyworld,_Orlando,_FL,_summer_1972_09.jpg. No copyright mark (PD image).

Disney Magic Kingdom. Source:

https://commons.wikimedia.org/wiki/File:Disneyland,_USA,_1977_(2).jpg. No copyright mark (PD image).

Trailer. Source: https://www.flickr.com/photos/91591049@N00/34844192056/in/photostream/ by SenseiAlan. Attribution 4.0 International. (CC by 4.0).

Family Camping. Source:

https://www.flickr.com/photos/bklbennett/3347459899/ by bklbennett. Attribution 4.0 International. (CC by 4.0)

The Youth of 1972:

Kids in classroom. Source: https://www.flickr.com/photos/lighttable/3919664210/in/photostream/ by Scott Clark. Attribution 4.0 International. (CC by 4.0).

Campus. Source: https://www.flickr.com/photos/euthman/2122302721/ by Ed Uthman. Attribution 4.0 International. (CC by 4.0).

Campus. Source: https://www.flickr.com/photos/euthman/2128366464/ by Ed Uthman. Attribution 4.0 International. (CC by 4.0).

Campus Students. Source:

https://commons.wikimedia.org/wiki/File:1970sgirls.jpg. No copyright mark (PD image).

Prom. Source:

http://setonhallhs.org/proms/1972/. No copyright mark (PD image).

Hippies performing at Pike Place Market. Source:

https://commons.wikimedia.org/wiki/File:Musicians_performing_at_Pike_Place_Market_anniversary_celebration,_1972.gif. No copyright mark (PD image).

Hippie Commune. Source:

http://www.tedpilger.com/sunnyridge/history/uploads/oldkitch.jpg. No copyright mark (PD image).

Peace Corps. Source:

http://peacecorpsonline.org/messages/messages/467/3332.html. No copyright mark (PD image).

Anti Vietnam War Paris. Source:

https://www.flickr.com/photos/13476480@N07/6940041190/in/photostream/ by manhhair. Attribution 4.0 International. (CC by 4.0).

Women's March No War. Source:

https://www.flickr.com/photos/dboo/5205309422/in/album-72157625122441513/ by Nick DeWolf. Rights Granted by © the Nick DeWolf Foundation

Marijuana. Source:

https://www.flickr.com/photos/usnationalarchives/3704385720/in/photolist-6DkWPj-6SQvo1-bLnF8a-6P7F3q-6DgL42-6DkUFW-7uX47H-bxs7GJ-6P3wpM-bF9xnJ-bSCnFH-6DkUEW-bU3PrX-bF9JrW-bU7r7B-bU3VoV-7vu1Pn-bSCcD4-6VwfXe-bLnvZx-73ZttY-6P3x5e-6P3zLe-7vbmLc-bSCoKr-bDGWmu-bDGQCo-bU69rF-72m9Nh-bSC8oF-6DkVe9-bDHSrf-6DgK4B-bSBW7r-6Pc9F1-73W1xg-6Vuk3x-6Vytyu-6DgNye-bU8CN6-SwQpkS-6DgJhT-bDHb6N-bFbtPG-9dhnqX-bDHA8C-6P7KCy-6VukXv-6DkTG3-bU43kH by The U.S National Archives. (PD Image).

World Events:

Nixon. Source:

https://en.wikipedia.org/wiki/Richard_Nixon. No copyright mark (PD image).

Nixon meets Mao. Source:

https://www.flickr.com/photos/13476480@N07/51231180943/in/photolist-2m48cea-6e1Ggz-EhXiQD-2m8Ehc7-2kDMbjC-Lhn7rt-eXj12u-97keFD-2kNXtXE-iCWEjF-BuVU2b-eX7hbv-ERqqW2-49HGS-k1H7g-BX4dBx-NyMorG-eXiR33-eX7xtZ-eX7tjn-iCWCLa-fEs9TL-2caMT63-ycAF8w-rZLG2-fEazsz-fEazKn-5uS672-q17ur5-8UukCe-fEazz4-9moxrU-xgugku-eX7cJz-BX4rFD-qLo1q2-683e1z-zgrtrv-29iZvnt-dTQ6Y-xVVDfh-6VHnk6-2Y7w5-eXj6Gh-UDQQVh-5ujqmN-iD1EvW-5sXtBu-xgwDGE-eX7BwF by manhhai. Attribution 4.0 International. (CC by 4.0).

Nixon and Ina. Source:

https://commons.wikimedia.org/wiki/File:Indira_and_Nixon.JPG. No copyright mark (PD image)

France Leader. Source:

https://en.wikipedia.org/wiki/Pierre_Trudeau. No copyright mark (PD image).

Vietnam War Collage. Source:

https://nara.getarchive.net/media/remembering-the-vietnam-war-8f48c1. No copyright mark (PD image).

Watergate Scandal Building. Source:

https://en.wikipedia.org/wiki/File:WatergateFromAir.JPG. No copyright mark (PD image).

Blue Marble. Source:

https://en.wikipedia.org/wiki/The_Blue_Marble#/media/File:The_Earth_seen_from_Apollo_17.jpg. No copyright mark (PD image).

Moon Landing. Source:

https://en.wikipedia.org/wiki/Apollo_17#/media/File:Apollo_17_Cernan_on_moon.jpg. No copyright mark (PD image).

Bloody Sunday. Source:

https://commons.wikimedia.org/wiki/File:Free_Derry_Bloody_Sunday_memorial_march.jpg. No copyright mark (PD image).

Bloody Sunday. Source:

https://commons.wikimedia.org/wiki/File:Free_Derry_Bloody_Sunday_memorial_march.jpg. No copyright mark (PD image).

Shoichi. Source:

https://en.wikipedia.org/wiki/Shoichi_Yokoi. No copyright mark (PD image).

Men supporting women rights. Source:

https://en.wikipedia.org/wiki/File:Warren_Farrell_leads_a_group_of_men_protesting,_1972.jpg. No copyright mark (PD image).

Munich Massacre. Source:

https://commons.wikimedia.org/wiki/File:Munich_massacre_memorial,_Tel_Aviv.JPG. No copyright mark (PD image).

Japan Winter Olympics. Source:

https://en.wikipedia.org/wiki/1972_Winter_Olympics#/media/File:Sapporo_1972_poster.png. No copyright mark (PD image).

Summer Olympic Germany Gold Medal. Source:

https://commons.wikimedia.org/wiki/File:Mary_Peters_1972_Olympic_gold_medal.JPG. No copyright mark (PD image).

HP-35 Calc. Source:

https://commons.wikimedia.org/wiki/File:HP-35_Red_Dot.jpg. No copyright mark (PD image).

Pong. Source:

https://en.wikipedia.org/wiki/Pong#/media/File:Signed_Pong_Cabinet.jpg. No copyright mark (PD image).

Polaroid Camera. Source:

https://commons.wikimedia.org/wiki/File:Polaroid_SX-70_(4462345243).jpg. No copyright mark (PD image).

Andy Warhol w/ polaroid. Source:

https://nara.getarchive.net/media/photograph-of-andy-warhol-taking-a-polaroid-picture-while-sitting-with-jack-ada90a. No copyright mark (PD image).

Fashion Trends:

3 friends men bell-bottoms

Wikipedia contributors. "1970s in Fashion." Wikipedia, 28 Sept. 2021, en.wikipedia.org/wiki/1970s_in_fashion#/media/File:Lars_Jacob_et_al_&_fashions_in_San_Diego_1971.jpg. No copyright mark (PD image).

Corduroy Bell Bottoms. Source:

https://commons.wikimedia.org/wiki/File:Moda_argentina_1972.png. No copyright mark (PD image).

Polka dot sweaters. Source:

https://www.flickr.com/photos/eklektikos/3860068933 by Todd Ehlers. Attribution 4.0 International. (CC by 4.0).

Black couple. Source:

https://en.wikipedia.org/wiki/1970s_in_fashion. No copyright mark (PD image).

Poco skirt. Source:

https://commons.wikimedia.org/wiki/File:Girl_in_Kensington_2.jpg. No copyright mark (PD image).

Disco Look. Source:

https://en.wikipedia.org/wiki/1970s_in_fashion#/media/File:Susana_Gim%C3%A9nez_1977_VII.jpg. No copyright mark (PD image).

Girls / Boy Ads. Source:

https://jezebel.com/the-best-sears-kids-fashions-for-spring-of-1972-5241161. Pre 1978, (PD* image).

Girls coming home from school. Source:

https://www.flickr.com/photos/usnationalarchives/3903971864/ by US National Archives. No copyright mark (PD image).

Teen boy ad. Source:

https://www.retrowaste.com/1970s/fashion-in-the-1970s/1970s-fashion-for-men-boys/. Pre 1978, (PD* image).

Women Ad. Source:

https://www.goretro.com/2015/11/selected-pages-from-1972-spiegel.html. Pre 1978, (PD* image).

Jeep Wrangler jeans. Source:

https://www.flickr.com/photos/jbcurio/2421803189 by Jamie. Attribution 4.0 International. (CC by 4.0). Attribution 4.0 International. (CC by 4.0).

Sweater Vests. Source:

https://www.boredpanda.com/1970s-mens-fashion-ads/?utm_source=google&utm_medium=organic&utm_campaign=organic. Pre 1978, (PD* image).

Women plaid outfits

"German Fashion." Wikipedia, 1972, commons.wikimedia.org/wiki/File:Bundesarchiv_Bild_183-L0902-114,_Leipzig,_Messe,_neue_Mode.jpg. No copyright mark (PD image).

Music & Entertainment:

Records on lawn. Source:

https://flickr.com/photos/euthman/1843060455/in/album-7215760287807187 by Ed Uthman. Attribution 4.0 International. (CC by 4.0).

TV Shows—

All in the Family. Source:

https://commons.wikimedia.org/wiki/File:All_In_the_Family_cast_1973.JPG. No copyright mark (PD image).

Stanford & Son. Source:

https://en.wikipedia.org/wiki/Sanford_and_Son. No copyright mark (PD image).

Hawaii Five 0. Source:

https://en.wikipedia.org/wiki/Hawaii_Five-O_(1968_TV_series,_season_4). No copyright mark (PD image).

Maude. Source:

https://en.wikipedia.org/wiki/Maude_Findlay. No copyright mark (PD image).

Bridget Loves Bernie. Source:

https://en.wikipedia.org/wiki/Bridget_Loves_Bernie. No copyright mark (PD image).

Family Band. Source:

https://commons.wikimedia.org/wiki/the_one_and_only,_genuine,_original_family_band. No copyright mark (PD image).

Mystery Movie. Source:

https://en.wikipedia.org/wiki/The_NBC_Mystery_Movie. No copyright mark (PD image).

MTM show. Source:

https://en.wikipedia.org/wiki/Mary_Tyler_Moore. No copyright mark (PD image).

Gunsmoke. Source:

https://www.flickr.com/photos/tom1231/4591075054. No copyright mark (PD image).

Ironside. Source:

https://en.wikipedia.org/wiki/Ironside_(1967_TV_series). No copyright mark (PD image).

Movies—

The Godfather. Source:

https://upload.wikimedia.org/wikipedia/commons/f/f4/The_Godfather_movie_logo.png. No copyright mark (PD image).

Poseidon Adventure. Source:

https://crazyfilmguy.blogspot.com/2014/04/the-poseidon-adventure-1972.html. Pre 1978, (PD* image).

What's up doc. Source:

https://www.en.wikipedia.org/wiki/What%27s_Up,_Doc%3F_(1972_film)#/media/File: What's_Up_Doc_poster.jpg. No copyright mark (PD image).

Deliverance. Source:

https://en.wikipedia.org/wiki/Deliverance. No copyright mark (PD image).

Jeremiah Johnson. Source:

https://en.wikipedia.org/wiki/Jeremiah_Johnson_(film). No copyright mark (PD image).

Cabenet. Source:

https://en.wikipedia.org/wiki/Cabaret_(1972_film). No copyright mark (PD image).

Deep Throat. Source:

https://en.wikipedia.org/wiki/Deep_Throat_(film). No copyright mark (PD image).

The Getaway. Source:

https://en.wikipedia.org/wiki/The_Getaway_(1972_film). No copyright mark (PD image).

Lady Sings the Blues. Source:

https://en.wikipedia.org/wiki/Lady_Sings_the_Blues_(film). No copyright mark (PD image).

Everything You've Always Wanted to Know about Sex. Source:

https://en.wikipedia.org/wiki/Everything_You_Always_Wanted_to_Know_About_Sex*_(* But_Were_Afraid_to_Ask)_(film). No copyright mark (PD image).

Music:

Robert Flack. Source:

https://en.wikipedia.org/wiki/Roberta_Flack. No copyright mark (PD image).

Neil Young. Source:

https://en.wikipedia.org/wiki/Greatest_Hits_(Neil_Young_album). No copyright mark (PD image).

Michael Jackson. Source:

https://en.wikipedia.org/wiki/Ben_(song). No copyright mark (PD image).

The Staple Singers. Source:

https://en.wikipedia.org/wiki/The_Staple_Singers. No copyright mark (PD image).

America. Source:

https://commons.wikimedia.org/wiki/Category:America_(band). No copyright mark (PD image).

https://commons.wikimedia.org/wiki/File:Gerry_Beckley_(America)_-_TopPop_1972_1.png. No copyright mark (PD image).

Al Green. Source:

https://en.wikipedia.org/wiki/Al_Green. No copyright mark (PD image).

ABBA. Source:

https://en.wikipedia.org/wiki/ABBA. No copyright mark (PD image).

https:/enwikipedia.org/wiki/File:ABBA_-Popzien_1973_5.png. No copyright mark (PD image).

Pink Floyd:

https://en.wikipedia.org/Pink_Floyd#media/File:ROCK_CONCERT._(FROM_THE_SITES_EXHIBITION_FOR_OTHER_IMAGES_IN_THIS_ASSIGNMENT_SEE_FICHE_NUMBERS_42,_97.)_-_NARA_-_553890.jpg. No copyright mark (PD image)

Ziggy Stardust. Source:

https://rockartfashion.net/2015/04/16/ziggy-stardust-platforms-are-back-and-not-only/ photographer unknown. Pre 1978 (PD image).

Tina Turner & Ike. Source:

https://commons.wikimedia.org/wiki/File:Ike_%26_Tina_Turner_231172_Dia14.jpg. No copyright mark (PD image).

Famous Birthdays:

Amanda Peet 1/11 American Actress. Source:

https://en.wikipedia.org/wiki/Amanda_Peet. No copyright mark (PD image).

Rob Thomas 2/14 American Singer/Songwriter. Source:

https://en.wikipedia.org/wiki/Rob_Thomas_(musician)#/media/File:Marisol_Thomas_Rob_Thomas_Shankbone_2010.jpg. No copyright mark (PD image).

Billie Joe Armstrong American Singer/Songwriter 2/17. Source:

https://commons.wikimedia.org/wiki/File:RiP2013_GreenDay_Billie_Joe_Armstrong_0004.JPG. No copyright mark (PD image).

Shaquille O'Neal Basketball Player 3/6. Source:

https://en.wikipedia.org/wiki/Shaquille_O%27Neal. No copyright mark (PD image).

Timbaland Producer/Rapper 3/10. Source:

https://en.wikipedia.org/wiki/Timbaland. No copyright mark (PD image).

Leslie Mann Actress 3/26. Source:

https://en.wikipedia.org/wiki/Leslie_Mann. No copyright mark (PD image).

Jennifer Garner 4/17 Actress. Source:

https://en.wikipedia.org/wiki/Jennifer_Garner. No copyright mark (PD image).

Carmen Electra 4/20 Actress & Model. Source:

https://commons.wikimedia.org/wiki/File:Carmen_Electra.jpg. No copyright mark (PD image).

Dwayne Johnson 5/2 (The Rock) Actor. Source:

https://en.wikipedia.org/wiki/Dwayne_Johnson. No copyright mark (PD image).

Notorious B.I.G Rapper 5/21. Source:

https://en.wikipedia.org/wiki/The_Notorious_B.I.G. No copyright mark (PD image).

Zinedine Zidane Soccer Player 6/23. Source:

https://en.wikipedia.org/wiki/Zinedine_Zidane. No copyright mark (PD image).

Maya Rudolf 6/27 Actress & Comedian. Source:

https://commons.wikimedia.org/wiki/File:Maya_Rudolph.jpg No copyright mark (PD image).

Sofia Vergara 7/10 Actress. Source:

https://en.wikipedia.org/wiki/Sof%C3%ADa_Vergara. No copyright mark (PD image).

Gerri Halliwell 8/6 Singer/Songwriter & Actress. Source:

https://en.wikipedia.org/wiki/Geri_Halliwell. No copyright mark (PD image).

Ben Affleck 8/15 Actor. Source:

https://en.wikipedia.org/wiki/Ben_Affleck. No copyright mark (PD image).

Cameron Diaz 8/30 Actress. Source:

https://en.wikipedia.org/wiki/Cameron_Diaz. No copyright mark (PD image).

Idris Elba 9/6 English Actor. Source:

https://en.wikipedia.org/wiki/Idris_Elba. No copyright mark (PD image).

Liam Gallagher 9/21 English Singer/Songwriter. Source:

https://en.wikipedia.org/wiki/Liam_Gallagher. No copyright mark (PD image).

Gwyneth Paltrow 9/27 Actress. Source:

https://en.wikipedia.org/wiki/Gwyneth_Paltrow. No copyright mark (PD image).

Dita Von Teese 9/28 Burlesque Performer. Source:

https://commons.wikimedia.org/wiki/File:Dita_Von_Teese_Cannes_2013.jpg. No copyright mark (PD image).

Marshall Mathers (Eminem) Rapper & Actor 10/17. Source:

https://commons.wikimedia.org/wiki/File:EMINEM_rapping_Anger_management_tour_2003.jpg. No copyright mark (PD image).

Brad Paisley Singer/Songwriter 10/28. Source:

https://en.wikipedia.org/wiki/Brad_Paisley. No copyright mark (PD image).

Jenny McCarthy Actress & Model 11/1. Source:

https://en.wikipedia.org/wiki/Jenny_McCarthy#/media/File:Jenny_McCarthy_2012.jpg. No copyright mark (PD image).

Claire Forlani Actress 12/17. Source:

https://en.wikipedia.org/wiki/Claire_Forlani. No copyright mark (PD image).

Jude Law Actor 12/29. Source:

https://en.wikipedia.org/wiki/Jude_Law. No copyright mark (PD image).

Sports:

Japan Olympics. Source:

https://en.wikipedia.org/wiki/1972_Winter_Olympics#/media/File:Sapporo_1972_poster.png. No copyright mark (PD image).

Yukio Kasaya Stamp. Source:

https://en.wikipedia.org/wiki/Yukio_Kasaya. No copyright mark (PD image).

Barbara Cochran. Source:

https://en.wikipedia.org/wiki/Barbara_Cochran#/media/File:Barbara_Cochran_1972cr.jpg . No copyright mark (PD image).

Summer Olympic Germany Gold Medal. Source:

https://commons.wikimedia.org/wiki/File:Mary_Peters_1972_Olympic_gold_medal.JPG. No copyright mark (PD image).

Mark Spitz. Source:

https://en.wikipedia.org/wiki/Mark_Spitz#/media/File:Mark_Spitz_1972.jpg. No copyright mark (PD image).

Olga Korbut. Source:

https://commons.wikimedia.org/wiki/File:Olga_Korbut_Milan_1972.jpg. No copyright mark (PD image).

Super Bowl 72. Source:

https://goldenrankings.com/SuperBowl6-C.htm. No copyright mark (PD image).

Hank Aaron. Source:

https://en.wikipedia.org/wiki/Hank_Aaron#/media/File:Hank_Aaron_1974.jpg. No copyright mark (PD image).

Summit Series. Source:

https://en.wikipedia.org/wiki/Summit_Series. No copyright mark (PD image).

"Yaz at the Plate." Flickr, 2012, www.flickr.com/photos/uconnbrowns/7383035196. (CC by 4.0)

Automobiles:

Buick Skylark 350. Source: https://www.flickr.com/photos/91591049@N00/30819250344/in/photolist-2hjsjmF-2kFjc6D-2fBa18H-pmHdB2-HW99KM-nuXFmf-puymFk-NXoHpf-omUS7W-yjRbcm-pwXL3Y-G9DkKn-2bMPySF-2hEgCJe-vh569C-ayp62s-aymoND-oXJ126-HWmVa6-pWFqXB-pWX7vf-7BJQbX-ojGkqm-FDh6ZF-pC6QHS-ANyBa7-o3eEQb-o3fXEi-2c8wnkT-2mb3XTP-pSkuGJ-pUr4aX-pUgepR-pSkuam-PEAvJw-2mzSZx3-w9LJie-7uahnt-p5eVgq-nso9AS-nsEcZM-8GW12F-dA9raw-8GW3xH-pfvmB2-nur7m4-bb7v5K-2hEjqHs-Wuz6GG-bzjbL2 by SenseiAlan. Attribution 4.0 International. (CC by 4.0).

Chrysler Newport Royal. Source:

https://www.flickr.com/photos/91591049@N00/31623834766/in/photostream/ by SenseiAlan. Attribution 4.0 International. (CC by 4.0).

1972 Chevrolet Monte Carlo. Source:

https://www.flickr.com/photos/91591049@N00/30819249924/in/photostream/ by SenseiAlan. Attribution 4.0 International. (CC by 4.0).

Oldsmobile '72. Source:

https://www.flickr.com/photos/135077409@N02/48965441098 by Ultramatic. No copyright mark (PD image).

1972 T2 Volkswagen Kobi. Source: https://commons.wikimedia.org/wiki/File:%2771_Volkswagen_Kombi_Camper_(Expo_VAQ_des_100_ans_de_Montr%C3%A9al-Nord).jpg. No copyright mark (PD image).

VW Camper. Source:

https://www.flickr.com/photos/ben30/218381075 by ben30. Attribution 4.0 International. (CC by 4.0).

Chevy Vega. Source:

https://www.flickr.com/photos/91591049@N00/13058212935/in/photostream/ by SenseiAlan. Attribution 4.0 International. (CC by 4.0).

Ford Cars Ranchero & Bronco. Source:

https://www.flickr.com/photos/91591049@N00/19984128219 by SenseiAlan. Attribution 4.0 International. (CC by 4.0).

Ford Mustang. Source: https://www.flickr.com/photos/91591049@N00/20053575745 by SenseiAlan. Attribution 4.0 International. (CC by 4.0).

Ford Mustang. Source: https://www.flickr.com/photos/915910449@N00/39262477490/in/photostream by SenseiAlan. Attribution 4.0 International. (CC by 4.0).

Jag. Source: https://www.flickr.com/photos/91591049@N00/13241727294 by SenseiAlan. Attribution 4.0 International. (CC by 4.0).

72 Porsche. Source: https://commons.wikimedia.org/wiki/File:Nationale_oldtimerdag_Zandvoort_2010,_1972_PORSCHE_911_T,_DR-94-25_pic1.JPG. No copyright mark (PD image). Attribution 4.0 International. (CC by 4.0).

BMW. Source:

https://www.flickr.com/photos/andreboeni/33308932035 by Andrew Bone. Attribution 4.0 International. (CC by 4.0).

Chevy Blazer. Source:

https://73-87.com/7387info/ads_GM/73_blazer_ad.jpg by 73-87. No copyright mark (PD* image).

https://www.flickr.com/photos/91591049@N00/19919038321/in/photostream by SenseiAlan. Attribution 4.0 International. (CC by 4.0).

Pontiac.

https://www.flickr.com/photos/91591049@N00/13901837647 by SenseiAlan. Attribution 4.0 International. (CC by 4.0).

Toyotas

https://flickr.com/photos/91591049@N00/39771555600/ by SenseiAlan. Attribution 4.0 International. (CC by 4.0).

Honda

https://flickr.com/photos/51764518@N02/23371440431 by Joe Haupt. Attribution 4.0 International. (CC by 4.0).

*Image from advertisement is under the public domain as it was published as a periodical issue (collective work) in the US between 1925 and 1977 without copyright notice attached to the advertisement

Family Life:

"1970s Travel | Lisa's Nostalgia Cafe." *Lisa's Nostalgia Cafe*, 2011, nostalgiacafe.proboards.com/thread/339/1970s-travel.

"A Brief History of Walt Disney World Ticket Price Increases." *Spectrum News 13*, 2015, www.mynews13.com/fl/orlando/news/2014/2/27/disney_ticket_price_history.

"CDC." *CDC*, 1972, www.cdc.gov/nchs/data.

Click Americana. "Look Back at These Vintage Fisher-Price Little People Play Sets & Remember the Good Ol' Days -." *Click Americana*, 7 May 2021, clickamericana.com/toys-and-games/fisher-price-little-people-sets.

Flores, Emy Rodriguez. "The Popular Vacation Spot the Year You Were Born." *Country Living*, 30 July 2020, www.countryliving.com/entertaining/g33409086/popular-vacations-when-born/?slide=22

"Orlando Sentinel - We Are Currently Unavailable in Your Region." *Orlando Sentinel*, 2018, www.tribpub.com/gdpr/orlandosentinel.com.

Rushing, Scotty. "Top 1972 Wedding Songs Loving You Could Never Be Better." *My Wedding Songs*, 8 Feb. 2021, www.myweddingsongs.com/weddingblog/1972-wedding-songs.

Wikipedia contributors. "Crissy." *Wikipedia*, 2 Dec. 2020, en.wikipedia.org/wiki/Crissy.

"Easy-Bake Oven." *Wikipedia*, 18 Sept. 2021, en.wikipedia.org/wiki/Easy-Bake_Oven.

"Kampgrounds of America." *Wikipedia*, 10 Sept. 2021, en.wikipedia.org/wiki/Kampgrounds_of_America.

"Toss Across." *Wikipedia*, 26 July 2020, en.wikipedia.org/wiki/Toss_Across.

"Uno (Card Game)." *Wikipedia*, 4 Dec. 2002, en.wikipedia.org/wiki/Uno_(card_game).

Wilcox, Bradford, et al. "The Evolution of Divorce." *National Affairs*, 2009, www.nationalaffairs.com/publications/detail/the-evolution-of-divorce.

The Youth of 1972:

"The 1970s Education: Overview | Encyclopedia.Com." *Encyclopedia*, www.encyclopedia.com/social-sciences/culture-magazines/1970s-education-overview. Accessed 31 Oct. 2021.

Bjerga, Alan. "May 1972: Antiwar Protests Become Part of U History." *The Minnesota Daily*, mndaily.com/188358/uncategorized/may-1972-antiwar-protests-become-part-u-history. Accessed 31 Oct. 2021.

Center, Nsc Research. "Current Term Enrollment- Fall 2015." *National Student Clearinghouse Research Center*, 28 Aug. 2020, nscresearchcenter.org/currenttermenrollmentestimate-fall2015.

Conflict Mn, Author. "Eight Days In May. Eight Days Of Rage. – Conflict Minnesota." *Conflict MN*, 15 July 2007, conflictmn.blackblogs.org/eight-days-in-may-eight-days-of-rage.

mediabest. "Steve Jobs Described His LSD Trips in College as '1 of the Most Important Things in My Life'" *Best Star News*, 4 June 2021, beststarnews.com/celebrities/steve-jobs-described-his-lsd-trips-in-college-as-1-of-the-most-important-things-in-my-life.

Times, The New York. "GALLUP FINDS RISE IN MARIJUANA USE." *The New York Times*, 6 Feb. 1972, www.nytimes.com/1972/02/06/archives/gallup-finds-rise-in-marijuana-use-51-of-college-students-say-they.html.

Wikipedia contributors. "Greenpeace." *Wikipedia*, 24 Oct. 2021, en.wikipedia.org/wiki/Greenpeace.

"Pell Grant." *Wikipedia*, 6 Oct. 2021, en.wikipedia.org/wiki/Pell_Grant.

World Events:

"5 Enduring Things About Apollo 17." *YouTube*, 20 Dec. 2017, www.youtube.com/watch?v=H4txfgy3z5Q&t=277s.

Wikipedia contributors. "Apollo 17." *Wikipedia*, 31 Oct. 2021, en.wikipedia.org/wiki/Apollo_17.

"Bloody Sunday (1972)." *Wikipedia*, 30 Oct. 2021, en.wikipedia.org/wiki/Bloody_Sunday_(1972).

"Equal Rights Amendment." *Wikipedia*, 26 Oct. 2021, en.wikipedia.org/wiki/Equal_Rights_Amendment.

"HP-35." *Wikipedia*, 20 Sept. 2021, en.wikipedia.org/wiki/HP-35.

"Japanese Holdout." *Wikipedia*, 11 Oct. 2021, en.wikipedia.org/wiki/Japanese_holdout.

"Munich Massacre." *Wikipedia*, 30 Oct. 2021, en.wikipedia.org/wiki/Munich_massacre.

"Polaroid SX-70." *Wikipedia*, 29 Aug. 2021, en.wikipedia.org/wiki/Polaroid_SX-70.

"Pong." *Wikipedia*, 18 Oct. 2021, en.wikipedia.org/wiki/Pong.

"Shoichi Yokoi." *Wikipedia*, 16 Sept. 2021, en.wikipedia.org/wiki/Shoichi_Yokoi.

"Vietnam War." *Wikipedia*, 31 Oct. 2021, en.wikipedia.org/wiki/Vietnam_War.

"Watergate Scandal." *Wikipedia*, 25 Sept. 2001, en.wikipedia.org/wiki/Watergate_scandal.

Fashion:

Boutique, Bitsy Bug. "A Look Back at Baby Clothes from the 1970's." *Kidizen*, 23 Jan. 2019, about.kidizen.com/2019/01/21/a-look-back-from-the-1970s.

Music & Entertainment:

Castelli, Luca. "Rolling Stone 500 Greatest Songs of All Time (2010 Version)." *Spotirama*, 1 Nov. 2021, spotirama.blogspot.com/2015/05/rolling-stone-500-greatest-songs-of-all.html.

"Song Facts." *Song Facts*, 2021, songfacts.com.

"The Story." *ABBA*, abbasite.com/story. Accessed 1 Nov. 2021.

Wikipedia contributors. "All in the Family." *Wikipedia*, 27 Oct. 2021, en.wikipedia.org/wiki/All_in_the_Family.

"Bridget Loves Bernie." *Wikipedia*, 3 Sept. 2021, en.wikipedia.org/wiki/Bridget_Loves_Bernie.

"Cabaret (1972 Film)." *Wikipedia*, 12 Oct. 2021, en.wikipedia.org/wiki/Cabaret_(1972_film).

"Deep Throat (Film)." *Wikipedia*, 7 Oct. 2021, en.wikipedia.org/wiki/Deep_Throat_(film).

"Disney Anthology Television Series." *Wikipedia*, 31 Oct. 2021, en.wikipedia.org/wiki/Disney_anthology_television_series.

"Everything You Always Wanted to Know About Sex* (*But Were Afraid to Ask) (Film)." *Wikipedia*, 7 Oct. 2021, en.wikipedia.org/wiki/Everything_You_Always_Wanted_to_Know_About_Sex*_(*But_Were_Afraid_to_Ask)_(film).

"Gunsmoke." *Wikipedia*, 13 Oct. 2021, en.wikipedia.org/wiki/Gunsmoke.

"Hawaii Five-O (1968 TV Series)." *Wikipedia*, 4 Oct. 2021, en.wikipedia.org/wiki/Hawaii_Five-O_(1968_TV_series).

"Ironside (1967 TV Series)." *Wikipedia*, 29 Oct. 2021, en.wikipedia.org/wiki/Ironside_(1967_TV_series).

"Jeremiah Johnson (Film)." *Wikipedia*, 23 Oct. 2021, en.wikipedia.org/wiki/Jeremiah_Johnson_(film).

"Lady Sings the Blues (Film)." *Wikipedia*, 28 Oct. 2021, en.wikipedia.org/wiki/Lady_Sings_the_Blues_(film).

"Maude (TV Series)." *Wikipedia*, 5 Oct. 2021, en.wikipedia.org/wiki/Maude_(TV_series).

"Sanford and Son." *Wikipedia*, 22 Oct. 2021, en.wikipedia.org/wiki/Sanford_and_Son.

"The Getaway (1972 Film)." *Wikipedia*, 21 Oct. 2021, en.wikipedia.org/wiki/The_Getaway_(1972_film).

"The Godfather." *Wikipedia*, 30 Oct. 2021, en.wikipedia.org/wiki/The_Godfather.

"The Mary Tyler Moore Show." *Wikipedia*, 25 Oct. 2021, en.wikipedia.org/wiki/The_Mary_Tyler_Moore_Show.

"The NBC Mystery Movie." *Wikipedia*, 14 Oct. 2021, en.wikipedia.org/wiki/The_NBC_Mystery_Movie.

"The Poseidon Adventure (1972 Film)." *Wikipedia*, 28 Oct. 2021, en.wikipedia.org/wiki/The_Poseidon_Adventure_(1972_film).

"What's Up, Doc? (1972 Film)." *Wikipedia*, 26 Oct. 2021, en.wikipedia.org/wiki/What%27s_Up,_Doc%3F_(1972_film).

Sports:

Wikipedia contributors. "1972 in Sports." *Wikipedia*, 16 Oct. 2021, en.wikipedia.org/wiki/1972_in_sports.

"1972 Miami Dolphins Season." *Wikipedia*, 30 Oct. 2021, en.wikipedia.org/wiki/1972_Miami_Dolphins_season.

"1972 Summer Olympics." *Wikipedia*, 14 Sept. 2021, en.wikipedia.org/wiki/1972_Summer_Olympics.

"1972 Winter Olympics." *Wikipedia*, 25 Sept. 2021, en.wikipedia.org/wiki/1972_Winter_Olympics.

"Barbara Cochran." *Wikipedia*, 6 July 2021, en.wikipedia.org/wiki/Barbara_Cochran.

"Hank Aaron." *Wikipedia*, 31 Oct. 2021, en.wikipedia.org/wiki/Hank_Aaron.

"Mark Spitz." *Wikipedia*, 15 Oct. 2021, en.wikipedia.org/wiki/Mark_Spitz.

"Olga Korbut." *Wikipedia*, 24 Oct. 2021, en.wikipedia.org/wiki/Olga_Korbut.

"Skiing Cochrans." *Wikipedia*, 5 Jan. 2021, en.wikipedia.org/wiki/Skiing_Cochrans.

"Summit Series." *Wikipedia*, 22 Oct. 2021, en.wikipedia.org/wiki/Summit_Series.

"Super Bowl VI." *Wikipedia*, 12 Oct. 2021, en.wikipedia.org/wiki/Super_Bowl_VI.

Automobiles:

Alan's Factory Outlet. "The 35 Cars With the Longest Production Runs of All Time | Custom Metal Garages and Carports." *Alan's Factory Outlet*, 9 Sept. 2021, alansfactoryoutlet.com/the-35-cars-with-the-longest-production-runs-of-all-time.

Brubaker, Ken. "1972 Chevy K5 Blazer - Four Wheeler Magazine." *MotorTrend*, 2 Sept. 2009, www.motortrend.com/how-to/129-0909-1972-chevrolet-k5-blazer.

"Buick Skylark | Classic Cars Wiki | Fandom." *Classic Cars Wiki*, classiccars.fandom.com/wiki/Buick_Skylark. Accessed 1 Nov. 2021.

"Chrysler Newport | Classic Cars Wiki | Fandom." *Classic Cars Wiki*, classiccars.fandom.com/wiki/Chrysler_Newport. Accessed 1 Nov. 2021.

"Cloudflare." *Cjponyparts*, www.cjponyparts.com/resources/ford-bronco-history. Accessed 1 Nov. 2021.

"Jaguar E-Type | Classic Cars Wiki | Fandom." *Classic Cars Wiki*, classiccars.fandom.com/wiki/Jaguar_E-Type. Accessed 1 Nov. 2021.

"Oldsmobile Cutlass | Classic Cars Wiki | Fandom." *Classic Cars Wiki*, classiccars.fandom.com/wiki/Oldsmobile_Cutlass#Fourth_Generation_-_1973.E2.80.931977. Accessed 1 Nov. 2021.

"Pontiac Grand Am | Classic Cars Wiki | Fandom." *Classic Cars Wiki*, classiccars.fandom.com/wiki/Pontiac_Grand_Am#1973.E2.80.931975. Accessed 1 Nov. 2021.

Wikipedia contributors. "Ford Bronco." *Wikipedia*, 27 Oct. 2021, en.wikipedia.org/wiki/Ford_Bronco.

"Ford Mustang." *Wikipedia*, 29 Oct. 2021, en.wikipedia.org/wiki/Ford_Mustang.

"Ford Ranchero." *Wikipedia*, 30 Sept. 2021, en.wikipedia.org/wiki/Ford_Ranchero.

"Honda Z." *Wikipedia*, 29 Sept. 2021, en.wikipedia.org/wiki/Honda_Z.

"Oldsmobile Cutlass." *Wikipedia*, 17 Oct. 2021, en.wikipedia.org/wiki/Oldsmobile_Cutlass#/media/File:1972_Oldsmobile_Cutlass_Supreme_Hardtop_--_10-19-2010.jpg.

"Toyota Corolla." *Wikipedia*, 30 Oct. 2021, en.wikipedia.org/wiki/Toyota_Corolla.

"Volkswagen Beetle." *Wikipedia*, 27 Oct. 2021, en.wikipedia.org/wiki/Volkswagen_Beetle.

"Volkswagen Type 2." *Wikipedia*, 4 Oct. 2021, en.wikipedia.org/wiki/Volkswagen_Type_2.

Printed in Great Britain
by Amazon

75332690R00095